WEST POINT
THE UNITED STATES MILITARY ACADEMY

WEST POINT
THE UNITED STATES MILITARY ACADEMY

DAVID PAHL

Exeter Books

NEW YORK

A Bison Book

Designed by Ruth DeJauregui
Edited by Timothy Jacobs and John Kirk

Acknowledgements
Many thanks to Arthur Alphin and Irwin Gold without whose generous assistance
this book would not have been possible.

Picture Credits
All photos courtesy of the Department of the Army except;
© Arthur Alphin: 30 (left), 30-31 (right), 36-37, 40 (top), 41 (top), 44 (bottom),
45 (top and bottom), 46, 47 (bottom), 56-57 (left), 73, 96 (top and bottom),
98-99 (left), 102-103, 106 (top left), 108-109, 110, 112 (bottom), 114-115, 118
(top), 120, 122-123 (right), 130, 134 (bottom left), 137 (bottom right), 139
(top and bottom)

Association of Graduates: 137 (top right), 140, 141
Ford Aerospace Communications Corp: 16 (bottom right)
Irwin Gold: 1, 12-13, 33, 58 (left), 58-59, 60, 61 (top), 62-63, 64, 74-75 (right),
82-83, 86, 101 (top), 104, 119, 122 (left), 126-127, 132-133 (left), 136-137
(left)
NASA: 69, 72, 76, 113
National Archives: 8 (bottom), 32 (bottom), 34-35 (right), 106-107 (right), 116-
117 (right)
United States Air Force: 116 (top left)
United States Department of Defense: 20 (top), 21, 61 (bottom right), 54
(top), 55 (lower right)
United States Military Academy: 10 (top right), 14-15, 16 (top), 28, 49 (top), 65,
67, 70-71, 78 (bottom left), 88 (top), 89 (top and bottom), 90-91, 92, 93 (top),
94-95, 100, 121, 129, 131
The White House (photograph by Michael Evans): 112 (top)

Page 1: Since 1976, women have been part of the Cadet Corps at the US Military
Academy. Though not yet as likely to be assigned to combat duty stations as men,
women partake , as do all cadets, of the Military Academy code: 'Duty—Honor—
Country.'

Page 2-3: Bearing a truly fortress-like appearance, the Central Cadet Barracks,
understandably a landmark on the West Point campus, suggests West Point's in-
ception in the late 18th century, when the 'Corps of Invalids' ('invalid' meaning,
at the time, something approximating 'nascent officer') was moved from its station in Philadelphia to the garrison at West Point, on the scenic and strategically
advantageous banks of the Hudson River.

This page: The Corps of Cadets is here assembled on 'the Plain,' in full drill formation. As highly regimented as this appears, it is said that, when walking on the
Academy grounds, one feels that one should literally 'breathe in march cadence.'

CONTENTS

THE ACADEMY

N orth of New York City, on the banks of the Hudson River, is the site of the United States Military Academy. This four-year professional school has the responsibility of educating, training and inspiring the men and women of the Corps of Cadets. Each graduate of the Academy is intended to have the character, leadership and intellectual foundation of an officer of the Regular Army of the United States.

The roots of the Academy may be traced all the way back to the American Revolution. In 1776 a proposal supported by George Washington and Alexander Hamilton suggested the establishment of a professional school to train military officers. In June of 1777, the Continental Congress created the Corps of Invalids which was to be employed for garrison and guard duty, and also to serve as a military school for young gentlemen previous to their being assigned to marching regiments.

By the end of the Revolutionary War, the Corps of Invalids had been moved to the garrison at West Point. The plan for the military school died from a lack of funds. For the next 20 years the school arose and died several times. It was finally a variety of external threats which demonstrated the need for a strong American military power to effectively deal with the world.

The origin of today's Military Academy can be found in an Act of Congress approved in March of 1802. During the previous years the Academy trained young men in ordinance and artillery manufacture as well as in engineering. The Act of 1802 essentially split this single Corps of Artillerists and Engineers into two separate Corps. The Corps of Engineers then at the school consisted of two officers and ten cadets. These people were ordered to remain at the school and would form the Military Academy. This Military Academy was placed under the supervision of the Secretary of War. The first class graduated in October of 1802.

This early version of the Military Academy suffered for a decade. There was little support for an Army, much less a military school. Further, the program at the Academy was irregular at best. Many cadets were authorized to attend but few actually got there. The instructors were active duty officers who rotated in and out of the Academy based on the needs of the Army. Ten years after the first class graduated, the Military Academy was in sure danger of being closed, but the War of 1812 changed its prospects.

Fearing war with England, the American Congress reorganized the Military Academy. By Act of Congress, the Academy was strengthened by improving operating regulations and toughening the requirements for admission. Further, rather than just graduating officers in the Corps of Engineers, Congress authorized the assignment

Opposite: **The Corp of Cadets color guard is on the march. In bygone eras of warfare, battle was essentially a series of one-on-one encounters, and having an intimidating personal appearance was important. Ergo, the horned helmets of ancient times, Indian warpaint and the traditional 'brush,' which is a form of plume, atop the cadet's parade hats, which are called 'shakos,' from the Hungarian root for 'pointed hat.'** *Above:* **A sculpted soldier gives the call to arms from the battle line of another era.**

of graduates to all branches of the Army. Congress also increased the faculty funding and established the post of Academy Superintendent. The Superintendent had responsibility for the Academy as well as the Post of West Point.

For the next five years the Academy improved but did not prosper. In 1817, the Academy's fortunes and prospects for the future changed. In 1817, Captain Sylvanus Thayer was appointed as Superintendent of the Academy. Captain Thayer's appointment was the turning point in the history of the United States Military Academy. Thayer was the 33rd graduate of the Academy in 1808. As superintendent nine years later, Thayer began many of the programs which still exist at the Academy today. Under Thayer, the Corps of Cadets was organized into a battalion.

Each cadet in the battalion received the training of a soldier, noncommissioned officer and an officer. Thayer's academic reforms included the establishment of a grading system and small classes for more intense training. The new programs were based on a foundation of scholarship, discipline, leadership, integrity and good character, and have found their way into the motto of the Military Academy, which is 'Duty, Honor, Country.'

Until the Civil War, the Academy served a two-fold purpose—as the national military school of the United States and as a school of engineering, but with the creation, via the Morrill Act in 1862, of the country's land grant colleges, the Academy's focus changed: that the cadets were engineers and officers—from all branches of the military.

By the end of the 1800s the Academy was upgraded somewhat—its facilities were modernized and its academic programs were improved, and the more concentrated military program focused on tactical field work, riding and physical conditioning. Also, these

Above: This is an aerial view of West Point on the scenic Hudson River. *Below:* The campaign hats worn in this photo date this group of Academy marksmen as cadets of the earlier twentieth century. Marksmanship practice is *de riguer* for cadets, who may someday become leaders of US Army infantry divisions. *Opposite:* Spit and polish, pride and the ability to handle a soldier's tools in trade are identifying characteristics of the well-rounded West Point cadet.

Right, inset: The Academy crest's 'Duty—Honor—Country' is the motto that West Point seeks to imprint on each cadet's heart as a lifelong guiding principle, and could well serve as a caption for this 20 September 1945 photo *(above)* of General of the Army (having five stars) Douglas MacArthur (West Point class of 1903) meditatively standing in Manila, the Philippines, after the long and very bloody Pacific campaign of World War II. MacArthur triumphantly fulfilled his prophetic, single-minded oath 'I shall return,' which was given as he and his staff were forced to flee the Japanese onslaught that captured the Philippines in the early days of the war. A very dedicated soldier, he was also a very dedicated student, consistently garnering marks for excellence at West Point.

In another photo of truly dutiful, brilliant soldiers, *(right)* Supreme Allied Commander, five-star General Dwight D Eisenhower *(immediate right)* is *here* greeted by *(left to right)* the brilliant and charismatic General George S Patton, Jr, Commander of the US Third Army; General Omar N Bradley, Commander of the 12th Army Group; and Lieutenant General Courtney Hodges, Commander of the US First Army. General (and later 34th President of the United States) Eisenhower belied his true career excellence by the almost archetypically American persona he presented: being a somewhat mediocre West Point cadet (class of 1915), he often referred to those of higher academic standing than he as 'file boners,' and threatened to quit the Academy out of 'sheer boredom.'

The legendary General George S Patton (class of 1909) also showed that one could 'straighten out and fly right,' as witnessed by his distinguished career after having been held back a year at the Academy due to 'academic deficiency.' General Omar N Bradley (class of 1915) eventually became the US Army Chief of Staff, and Lieutenant General Courtney Hodges had a successful career after a shakey start: he was dismissed from West Point in 1905 for flunking geography. He gained an Army officer's commission by competitive examination in 1909. Partially due to the 'officer crunch' of World War I, and due in part to his honorable service during that war, he rose to the rank of major and his career stabilized into an upward mode. It might be said that he seldom had any real trouble finding his way around, but it may be fortunate that he wasn't in command of a bomber squadron. If these histories belie the worth of an Academy military education, let us not forget 'the class the stars fell on,' Eisenhower and Bradley's West Point class of 1915: almost 40 percent of the 164 cadets who graduated that year went on to become generals, and many of whom would serve with wisdom and honor in the greatest human conflict of recorded history—World War II. *Overleaf:* An upperclassman benefits from 'wisdom handed down' as an advisor lends him tempering words of experience.

waning years of the last century saw initiation of the Cadet Honor Code and the Cadet Honor Committee.

During the first decade of the twentieth century curriculum was liberalized to include courses in social sciences and languages, and during the first fifteen years of this century, some of the most famous graduates of the Academy were cadets. Douglas MacArthur graduated in 1903, and the class of 1915 was dubbed 'the class the stars fell on.' Of the 164 cadets who graduated in that year, almost 40 percent became generals. The class produced two Generals of the Army (Omar Bradley and Dwight Eisenhower). There were also two four star generals, seven three star generals, 24 two star generals and 24 one star generals. Bradley became the first Chairman of the Joint Chiefs of Staff and—of course—Eisenhower became the 34th President of the United States.

Above: **Despite millenia of military evolution, armies remain at heart what has become known as 'infantry,' which word, while it springs from the same root as 'infant,' means 'young foot soldiers' such as these arriving at Osan Army Base, Korea for the Team Spirit '85 War Games—and not 'babes in the woods.' The same goes for these cadets** *(right)* **training on the extensive West Point campus. The object held by the soldier** *at right* **probably ain't an umbrella.**

World War I strained the Academy programs almost to the breaking point. The demand for more officers resulted in abbreviated courses and curriculum descriptions, lowering of standards and early graduations. The Academy slipped from a professional program to little more than an officer's candidate school, producing about a class a year. Not until Douglas MacArthur, who had, in 1930, become Chief of Staff of the US Army, was able to see the need for an expansion of the program did this situation change. He added new technical subjects, expanded extracurricular activities and an intramural athletic program. By 1933, the United States Military Academy was authorized to confer the bachelor of science degree upon those cadets who complete the four year program.

By World War II, the Academy needed to expand to again fill the need for field officers. The Academy program was expanded to include pilot training, and the demand for officers in all areas resulted in a series of improvements which have made the Academy the complex and efficient educational institution that it is today.

The Military Academy is only the beginning for an Army cadet. Graduates of the Academy are commissioned as second lieutenants in the Regular Army and will be assigned to one of a wide variety of career specialties. We will digress a bit to briefly cover each of these career fields.

When people think of the Army they usually think of the Infantry. This branch forms the backbone of our Army. Infantry officers serve as platoon and company commanders, counselors of men and as staff officers buried in the paperwork of responsibility. This is one of the two army career specialties which are not open to women.

Above: An M60 main battle tank halts its 57-ton ramble during West Point Armor maneuvers at Fort Knox—par for the Academy's 'first you learn about it, then you use it,' approach to education. *Immediate right:* The sun shines through the Chaparral short-range air defense missile system. *Opposite:* Named for General Creighton Abrams, (Academy class of 1936), the 60-ton M1-A1 main battle tank is capable of speeds up to 45mph. Academy graduates going into the Armor specialty learn the tactical deployment of these and other armored vehicles.

Today what used to be called Cavalry is represented by a special branch of the Army called Armor. Armor includes the Armored Cavalry, Air Cavalry, Armor, Attack Helicopter Squadron and the Air Cavalry Combat Brigade. The Armor officer develops the capability of employing tanks, Armored and Air Cavalry, Mechanized Infantry, Artillery, Engineers and Army Aviation. Like Infantry, this career specialty is not open to women.

Field Artillery is the next career area we will consider. Today's Field Artillery officer is trained to know how to use such high technology systems as laser range finders, remotely piloted vehicles, multiple rocket launchers and large caliber howitzers. The officer with this specialty knows about battle plan formulation, proficiency and tactical expertise.

An AH-64 Apache attack helicopter *(above)* looms large for Academy graduates being commissioned second lieutenants in the Army Aviation career specialty. Shown here armed with Hellfire missiles, the AH-64 is a very effective tank destroyer, and is also used to disrupt enemy invasive action until 'friendly' forces can join in the fray. Equipped with integrated helmet sights for its missiles, 30mm cannon and 2.75-inch rockets, as well as laser range finder and laser target designator for the Hellfire missile system and an infrared night vision sensor, the Apache would be capable of making any enemy 'circle their wagons.'

In today's world of ballistic missiles and supersonic strike aircraft, defense of airspace is critical. The Army career specialty of Air Defense Artillery is an extremely important field. Officers learn about such defense systems as Patriot, Hawk, Nike, Hercules and many others. The officers in this field will likely play an increasingly important role in the defense of our country.

Every aspiring officer probably thinks at least a little bit about the Aviation career specialty. Officers in this specialty play key roles in such areas as combat, combat support, communication and intelligence operations. Army aviators fly transport helicopters, gunships and medivac ships. The challenges in this area are many, and many cadets consider Aviation as the most exciting specialty.

The original Academy program was for the Corps of Engineers. Engineer officers are responsible for training and leading troops in combat and construction essential to the Army in the field. Engineering officers are trained in the areas of civil works, cartography, surveying, bridge construction and environmental studies.

Although the Military Police are trained to take care of routine police duties, they are also responsible for determining potential enemy disruption of communications in time of war. Their training includes physical security, combat tactics and combat support.

Every army must have some sort of intelligence corps to figure out what an opponent intends to do. This is the job of the Military Intelli-

Left: **Airborne training is probably not like 'falling off a log.'** *Below:* **Upon graduation, cadets may be commissioned for a career in the Military Police, who are responsible for routine police activities and, in time of war, for detecting enemy disruption of communications.** *Right:* **The 1st and 2nd Battalions of the Army's 75th Infantry parachute onto Grenada's Point Salines Airfield, in the Grenada invasion of 25 October 1983. Graduates may find careers in ordering men to do this—and in joining them as they do it.**

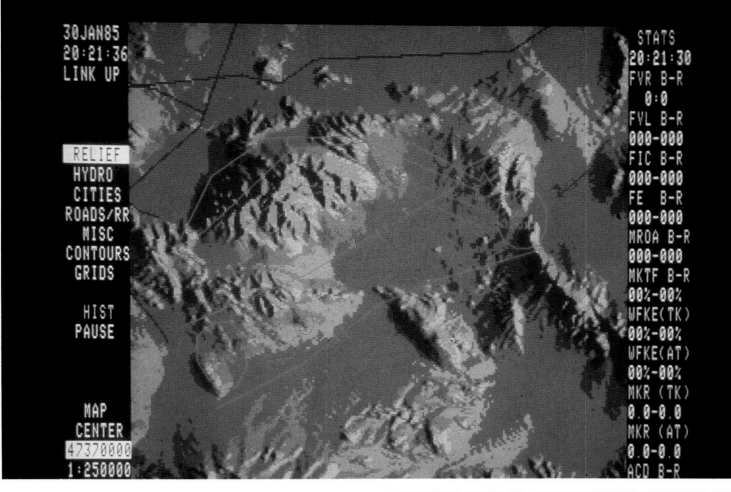

Left and right : **The newly-commissioned Army second lieutenant in the Chemical Warfare specialty may find his uniform and training peculiar at times. In this ragingly controversial service branch, the fresh West Point graduate will learn battlefield survival techniques, intelligence procedures, offensive and defensive measures and weapons support for nuclear, biological and chemical warfare operations. A computer-enhanced Army intelligence map of a tactical 'theater' is shown** *above.*

gence career specialty. This is one of the largest branches of the Army—with duties ranging from intelligence, security, counterintelligence, cryptology and signal intelligence to interrogation, aerial surveillance and planning. The officers in this field are all engaged in the constant battle of gathering, analyzing and disseminating intelligence data. To do this, officers are trained to work with radio intercept equipment, computers and satellites.

Army relies heavily upon communications. Officers with a specialty in the Signal Corps are responsible for the communications which keep the Army on the move.

There are about 800,000 people in today's Army, and the organization designed to manage such a large entity is the Adjutant General Corps. This career field actually runs the Army, managing personnel, post office and even the Army band. These are the people who 'hold the Army together.'

There is one career specialty which is small and, when one considers it, very scary. This is the career field of Chemical Warfare. The officer in this area learns about chemical and nuclear weapons employment support, defensive procedures, fallout prediction and battlefield survival techniques, as well as intelligence aspects of nuclear, biological and chemical warfare operations.

In the Army, as with any other organization, nothing happens unless something moves. The Transportation career specialty is the business of moving things and people. Officers learn planning, pro-

curement and the coordination and control measures necessary to move people and equipment by way of air, rail, water and highways.

If nothing happens unless something moves, then it follows that people will not work unless they are paid. The Finance Corps career specialty is responsible for pay, travel and transportation allowances, disbursement of public funds and many other other financial systems. The officers in the Finance Corp are responsible for controlling funds which total millions of dollars.

The Quartermaster career specialty is involved with basic supplies—food, petroleum and spare parts. Officers in this area are involved in one of three specialties: Subsistence management, Material/Service management, or Petroleum management.

The officer involved in the Ordinance specialty is concerned with combat material in four categories: ammunition (both conventional and nuclear); weapons (small arms all the way up to artillery); vehicles (from trucks to tanks); and missiles of all types.

There are three specialties in the Army which are essentially unique. These are Special Forces, the Rangers and the Airborne. Qualified officers participate in rigorous and often dangerous training programs designed to test their endurance, strength and character. Those involved in Airborne and Ranger training also have one of the specialties described previously. In the Special Forces, officers could undergo more than a year in training for counterinsurgency and unconventional warfare operations.

Before even considering any of these specialties however, a prospective candidate must earn a degree and commission at an extremely demanding school. Now that we know a little about the history of the school and the possibilities of a interesting career in the Army, it is time to learn about what it takes to overcome the challenge of the United States Military Academy.

The Rangers are a unique service branch open to qualified officers who can make it through the rugged Ranger training. West Point graduates may find themselves in for a tougher time than Beast Barracks, as the US Army Rangers are called upon to be advance patrols *(left)*, perform heavy-camouflage combative duty deep within enemy territory *(below)* and the occasional 'lone Ranger' may find himself being the sole reconnaissnce and sabotage man dropped off in hostile territory *(overleaf)*. Rangers performed rugged duty in Vietnam, and were the shock troops for the Grenada invasion.

THE PROFESSIONAL LIFE OF A CADET

The Military Academy requires a significant investment by not only its students but also its faculty. In order to more fully understand the life of a student, we must first understand the makeup of the faculty.

When visiting the Academy one is struck with the impression that everyone is in the military, which is close to the truth: almost the entire faculty of the Academy is made up of military personnel. Administrative titles at the Academy are different from most colleges but job functions are similar. The chief executive of the school is the Superintendent. This position is much like that of a college president. However, the Superintendent is also the Commander of the military post at West Point, which post was first established in 1777, and is now the oldest continuously operated military installation in the United States. Reporting to the Superintendent is the Chief of Staff, who is the principal decision maker in matters of installation management and community affairs. The Chief of Staff works at improving the effectiveness, economy, responsiveness and quality of support and services provided to all elements of the Military Academy.

Also reporting to the Superintendent is the Dean of the Academic Board, who, much like a college dean of faculty, coordinates the activities of the academic departments and advises the Superintendent on all academic matters.

Finally, we have the Commandant of Cadets—the military Academy equivalent of a Dean of Students, who oversees the student government as well as supervises the military training of the Corps of Cadets.

The Superintendent, Dean of the Academic Board and the Commandant of Cadets form the core of the Academic Board of the Military Academy. The other members of the Board include the 13 department heads of the various academic disciplines: the Director of Admissions, the Director of Military Instructions, the Director of Physical Activity and the Medical Activity Commander. This Academic Board is responsible for such basic policy formulation as standards for admissions, academic performance minimums and a wide range of other educational and administrative policies.

The remaining faculty is almost entirely military personnel, being comprised of more than 500 Army, Air Force and Navy officers of the United States Armed Forces. Most faculty members have six to nine years of military experience in a variety of assignments, including approximately two years as graduate students prior to their assignments to the Academy. In addition, there are also four officers from allied countries. Of the total faculty there are 15 civilian professors of general subjects, four civilian foreign language professors

General Dwight D Eisenhower, a statue of whom *(left)* is situated cater-cornered to landmark Bartlett Hall *(in the background)*, was one of five World War II US generals (including generals Marshall, Arnold, Bradley and MacArthur) commissioned as five-star 'Generals of the Army,' second in rank only to World War I 'General of the Armies' John J Pershing. *Above:* The entire Corps of Cadets is shown *here* in review formation on 'the Plain.'

and approximately 20 civilian physical education instructors.

More than three-quarters of the faculty have earned masters degrees and, of that group, nearly one-quarter hold doctorates in their respective fields of endeavor. Perhaps the most interesting statistic about the Military Academy is the fact that almost 70 percent of the Regular Army officers on the faculty are also graduates of the Academy. This fact gives the students a unique advantage—not only do the instructors know their subjects but they are also well aware of the demands put upon the cadets.

Above: Then-Major Arthur Alphin gives a lecture on Armor technology. The majority of Academy instructors are Regular Army officers—a system anchored in the fundamental revisions made to Academy regimen by 'the Father of the US Military Academy,' West Point Superintendent (1817-1833) Sylvanus Thayer. *Right:* Cadets with their studies in mind crowd eponymously-named Thayer Road—which fronts Bartlett Hall *(on left)*—passing an MP *(center).*

The Military Academy is very concerned with the continuity of the academic program. The majority of instructors at the Academy are Regular Army officers, and are transferred after one three-to four-year tour of duty there—so the problem of continuity is resolved by tenured faculty. There are nearly 76 tenured members of the West Point faculty; 24 are professors and the remainder are associate professors. Full professors are appointed by the President of the United States, based upon the recommendation of the Academic Board. These professors serve as heads or deputy heads of academic departments and are generally well recognized within their fields of endeavor. Permanent associate professors are appointed by the Secretary of the Army, again based upon the recommendation of the Academic Board. Full and associate professors are allowed to remain at West Point until they have completed 30 years of active duty.

As a college a board of trustees, the Academy has a distinguished Board of Visitors, which is responsibe for the annual review of the Academy. Curriculum, policies, equipment and facilities are included in this review, which is submitted to the President of the United States. The Board of Visitors is made up of 12 people; six of whom are appointed by the President of the United States, and six who are appointed by Congress.

The faculty and Board look to the professional development of the Corps of Cadets. The very first aspect of this development involves

the concept of honor. An early superintendent of the Military Academy, Sylvanus Thayer, firmly believed that the school should produce leaders whose foundation was built on honor integrated with a strong sense of discipline. From those early days of the Academy to the present, the honor system has been an integral part of the program.

Douglas MacArthur was instrumental in formalizing the Honor Code and the Honor System. He was also the moving force in making the Honor System and Code an officially sanctimonial element of the Academy program.

The Honor Code is eloquent in its simplicity: it states that 'a cadet will not lie, cheat, or steal nor tolerate those who do.' In short, every cadet is expected—indeed required—to tell the truth on all occasions.

The Honor System includes the teaching of the Code, and is also the method by which the Code is enforced. The Cadet Honor Committee, elected from companies from within the Corps of Cadets, is charged with the responsibility for the administration, education and enforcement of the Code.

The Honor Committee's education of new cadets in the principles of the Honor Code is continuous and intensive. It includes informal discussions as well as scheduled lectures, in which it becomes apparent to all new cadets that all members of the Corps share a common

Right: At the end of their first day at the Academy, plebes swear allegiance to the United States, and to US Army procedures. *Below:* In this 1951 photo, then-president of France Vincent Auriol is honored with the 'Band Box Review' on the Central Cadet Barracks' interior courtyard. *Opposite:* The West Point marching uniform is based in the 19th century, from the Academy crest on the cadet's shako (aka 'tar bucket') to his brilliantly polished shoes.

pride in the Code as the cornerstone of the developmental program for all cadets.

Of course, the Code is not all of the training which new—or fourth class—cadets receive. Their first introduction to the academy is very likely the biggest cultural shock of their young lives. In just a few short (but seemingly unending) weeks, new cadets are transformed from civilians into prospective officers of the United States Army.

In July of each year, a new fourth class is admitted to the Academy. The first week is a blur of activity. Forms must be completed—only the government can possibly have so many forms to fill out. Each new cadet—or 'plebe' as first-year students are also known—must pass through the uniform issue lines and take physical examinations. The days are filled with a never ending list of things to do. No

Above: **These newly-arrived students betray a wide variety of apprehensions.** *Below:* **Prospective cadets must pass, in addition to academic tests, a Physical Aptitude Test comprised of pullups (for men) or flexed arm hangs (for women), a standing long jump, a kneeling basketball throw and a 300-yard shuttle run.** *Right:* **The West Point campus has many facilities and playing fields, such as this baseball diamond photographed in 1944, to encourage cadet physical fitness.** *Overleaf:* **This is a view up 'C ramp' to the massive Cadet mess hall building, aka Washington Hall.**

Left: **A plebe is an Academy student equivalent to a civilian freshman. Tumbling backward into a pool of water demands calm collectedness on the part of the fully field-dressed plebe, who performs this action repeatedly as part of 'confidence obstacle course training.' After their first June break, plebes enter a new class year, are now known as 'yearlings' and report to West Point's Camp Buckner *(above)*—to practically apply their classroom knowledge in fatiguing simulated tactical situations. Then they visit Fort Knox, Kentucky for a one-week course in Armored operations.**

doubt many plebes wonder what they're doing there. There is one brief moment to reflect however. This comes when it is time to take the oath of office. Each new cadet is sworn in with the following words:

'I solemnly swear that I will support the Constitution of the United States, and bear true allegiance to the National Government; that I will maintain and defend the sovereignty of the United States paramount to any and all allegiance, sovereignty, or fealty I may owe to any state or country whatsoever; and that I will at all times obey the legal orders of my superior officers, and the Uniform Code of Military Justice.'

With these words each individual begins their term as a cadet and looks forward to the next oath, to be taken four years later, which is the oath of office of a commissioned officer in the Regular Army of the United States.

With this oath, Cadet Basic Training officially begins. This six and one-half week training program is so difficult that the cadets are not allowed to quit! This period, called 'Beast Barracks' by all who have gone through it, is the most physically and emotionally demanding part of the entire four year program at West Point.

Above: The average plebe's 'quarters,' where study and sanctuary are found. *Below:* An upperclassman makes sure that these plebes are 'spit and polish' inside and out. *Upper opposite:* These cadets polish off an urn of coffee as they plot trajectories in an ordnance lab session. The insignia in stained glass at *lower opposite,* worn by upperclassmen: Pallas Athene's helmet (for wisdom and learning) over a Greek sword (for the military profession).

A typical daily schedule during Beast Barracks proceeds as follows:

0600	Reveille
0600 - 0730	Physical Training
0730 - 0755	Personal Maintenance
0800 - 0845	Breakfast
0900 - 1245	Training and Classes
1300 - 1345	Lunch
1400 - 1545	Training and Classes
1600 - 1730	Organized Athletics
1730 - 1755	Personal Maintenance
1800 - 1845	Dinner
1900 - 2100	Training and Classes
2100 - 2200	Personal Time
2200	Taps - lights out

The new cadets are hurried through the days. There is much to learn and only six and one-half weeks in which to become completely familiar with both Academy and Army procedure. Almost 80 percent of the Beast Barracks summer is devoted to training. The remaining 20 percent of the scheduled time is set aside for administrative efforts.

The first of four basic training categories during Beast Barracks, military training includes rifle and pistol qualification; first aid; tactics; Rand navigation; nuclear, biological and chemical defenses; and traditional army marching drills, ceremonies and military customs.

The second Cadet Basic Training area is in the military social graces—etiquette, and what may be considered stress management classes. Each cadet also learns about the campus, the various facilities of the school and the history of the Military Academy.

The Military Academy has very strict standards for physical fitness and each cadet is expected to successfully meet the challenge. The Physical Training effort involves physical conditioning and testing, as well as organized athletics. The program includes long marches, a leadership reaction course and what's known as a confidence obstacle course. The plebes learn to press themselves to the limit of their endurance during these physical training sessions.

The final area covered during the first summer at the Academy is that of Moral and Ethical Training. During these sessions the new cadets learn about the Honor Code and Honor System, and about the regulations pertaining to each cadet.

The four training categories are the core of Beast Barracks. The remainder of a new cadet's time is spent on academic and administrative work: plebes must be placed in the proper schedule of

Academy military training involves marching drills, and special unit formations such as this saber guard *(right)*, marching on the quad of Washington Hall. On graduation day, the Brigade Staff—the heads of the Corps—don their dress uniforms and form such a saber guard during the graduation day parade. Howitzers and anti-aircraft guns use prismatic sights, shown *above* being homed in by a cadet, whose two buddies attend the procedure, under a ceiling of camouflage net—*de riguer* for field batteries.

classes, have their previous course work validated and receive their books and supplies in time for the regular academic program of the Academy, which begins in late August. Freshmen must also receive the uniform and military equipment required to be a plebe at the Academy.

The fourth class system becomes the way of life for the new Academy cadet. It prescribes almost every facet of a new cadet's day during the tough Beast Barracks summer, and has, at its core, three fundamental parts: first, the system prescribes the relationship between upperclass cadets and the new plebes. This relationship is really quite simple: a plebe is lower than every other class, and each plebe is constantly reminded of this often frustrating fact of life. Second, the system defines the authorizations by which each plebe must live while at West Point. Again, the rules are quite straightforward: there are very few privileges enjoyed by plebes, and there are all sorts of restrictions. The third fundamental requirement of the fourth class system is that each plebe learns specific historical and contemporary Academy-related information with precision.

Throughout that first tough summer each new cadet must not lose perspective. The mission of the United States Military Academy is to educate plebes to be commissioned officers in the Regular Army of the United States. The cornerstone of this education and training may be summed up in one word: discipline. The daily regimen of cadet life, particularly at Cadet Basic Training, is designed to develop an appreciation for discipline and the need to maintain a professional standard of the highest order. Cadets learn self-discipline and sensitivity to the needs of others. Cadets also quickly discover that they must constantly make an extra effort in order to succeed. They learn how to manage their time and to establish priorities in order to stay on top of their work load.

The cadets cannot do all of this on their own. The Academy staff is structured to provide support for every cadet. The Commandant of Cadets is supported by four Regimental Tactical Officers who supervise the Corps of Cadets. Each tactical officer acts as a leader, supervisor and counselor to the more than 100 cadets in each of 36 cadet companies, and is an experienced Army officer who is directly responsible for company training, administration, morale and discipline. More specifically, the tactical officer's responsibilities to each cadet include the following: the 'tac' must encourage the cadets to work to their full potential; he must carefully review the performance of each cadet; he must select and recommend outstanding ca-

dets for positions of responsibility; he must be ready at all times to counsel individual cadets and to help in any way possible to resolve personal problems; and he is a liaison between the cadets and their parents whenever necessary.

In mid-August the new cadets who successfully completed the summer basic training are formally accepted into the corps. During the ceremonies on this day, these new members of the corps are able to relax and be satisfied in their achievement. They are congratulated for having the fortitude to complete a very difficult period in their lives.

Following 'R-day' it is business as usual, and the plebes must hurry into the next phase of life at the Academy. First on the list is room assignment. Each cadet is assigned to one of the 36 companies which make up the corps. Then roommates are assigned. Roommates are always members of the same company. Cadets are generally assigned three to a room and assignments are based on three considerations. First all roommates are to be of the same sex. Second, academic strengths and weaknesses are considered. Plebes who are weak in one subject area are matched with others who are strong in that same subject. In this way, the cadets can help one another through the rigors of the Academy.

The third consideration is personality. No matter how carefully cadets may be screened, there is always the possibility of personality conflicts. Room assignments take into consideration this sort of interpersonal friction.

Once assigned to rooms, the plebes keep their roommates for the first semester. Following that, room assignments are changed for the second half of the year. This sort of movement encourages the cadets to mingle and fosters a sense of camaraderie within a specific company of the corps.

During the freshman year, all plebes must take two military science courses besides their academic courses. The first is an introduction to the military profession. This course not only introduces the

Above: This cadet demonstrates time efficiency by studying while on indoor guard duty. *Below:* In this 1970 photo, cadet Ken Karhuse butters up the Commander's dog. *Upper right:* A view of the interior court of the Central Cadet Barracks, which is one of several cadet barracks at West Point. *Lower right:* Even West Point cadets are tempted to play—as 'horsing around' is tonic for the Army 'mule' (the school's name animal and football mascot). *Here,* physical education students engage in a shower-stuffing project. *Note* the upperclass insignia on the cadet *at center's* sleeve.

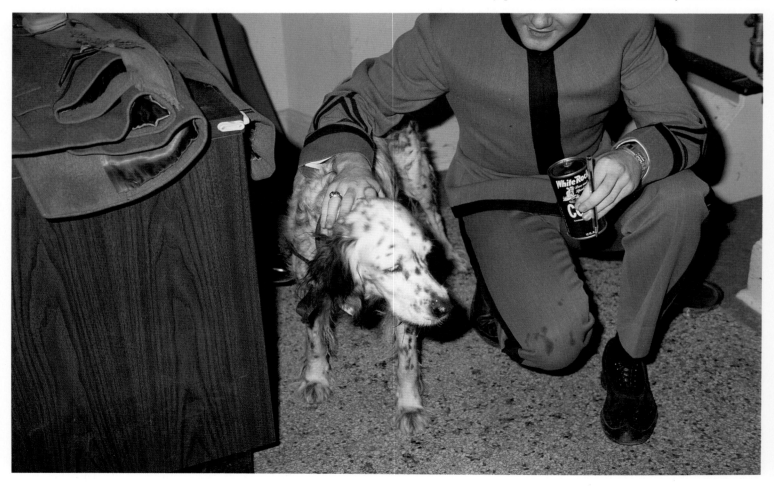

plebe to the military, it also analyzes the military from a technical, ethical and personal point of view. The course also looks at the military profession in the context of American culture. Finally, this course examines current world and national issues which affect the role of the United States Military. This course is intended to help each student understand their own values as a part of the United States Military establishment.

The second military science course provides the opportunity for cadets to look at a battlefield situation as would an infantry platoon leader. Three essential categories of officer skills are learned in this way: map reading, small unit tactical planning and oral communications. Cadets learn to combine these three skills in order to plan, organize and execute small unit combat operations. These operations range from point defense to deliberate attack. By the time the course is complete, the plebes have an excellent understanding of the methods by which a platoon leader can achieve an objective. Further, and just as important, the cadets have learned how to communicate their wishes in the form of clear and precise language.

The first year at the Military Academy is tough. Plebes spend almost ten months being junior to just about everyone at the school. Although there are many milestones at the Academy, perhaps one of the biggest comes in May. In May, the first classmen graduate and all of the remaining classes are 'promoted.' In May the plebes are promoted to third class! They have survived to now be recognized as upper class cadets. The celebration also signals one other important event: Summer vacation!

Time moves swiftly though, and after their June vacation the third class cadets report back to school. This time they report to Camp Buckner, which is located on the 16,000 acre West Point Reservation, for seven weeks of military field training. The training during these weeks is designed to be mentally and physically demanding. The cadets are stressed in order to simulate critical situations. The

As part of an overall educational approach, West Point acquaints its cadets with both old and new. Cadets can become functionally knowledgeable about the Thompson submachine gun *(left)* (this one circa 1929); implant a seed in themselves—of what may become professional Airborne training—aboard a Bell UH-1 Iroquois helicopter *(above,* flying by the Academy); and participate in an instructional film on the tactical operation of 19th century cannon *(below).*

Part of combat training is the setting and detecting *(above)* of land mines. This traditionally touchy business is probably one of the few times you'd feel ambivalent about finding 'unexpected treasure.' Part of any military operation is getting the equipment there—the two soldiers shown *below* are lifting anchoring hooks out of their bays to secure heavy vehicles to the bed of a transport barge, upon which these fellows are kneeling. Other aspects of 'soldiering knowhow' are the arts of camouflage *(above right)*; deployment of such vehicles as the M-1 Abrams main battle tank *(below right)*; and the vertiginous art of rapelling *(overleaf)*—all of which, as future officers, cadets must know, in order to know their tactical capabilities.

training is a mix of real army operations. Cadets learn more about infantry operations. Drawing from their studies in the plebe year they apply what was learned in somewhat more advanced situations. They also learn about artillery firing, weapons training, military engineering and field communications. As if this is not enough, the cadets are given a course in mountaineering skills and survival. The training is intense and cadets are challenged to stretch themselves to the limit of their endurance to keep up.

There is some free time at Camp Buckner. During the off duty hours, cadets have an opportunity to relax somewhat in preparation for the days of training yet to come. Camp Buckner facilities include such pleasantries as swimming, sailing and canoeing for recreation.

Once the Camp Buckner experience is complete the cadets are sent to Fort Knox, Kentucky for one more period of intensive training before the school year begins. This training at Fort Knox is a one-week crash course. Cadets receive a basic familiarization course in armor, the cavalry, mechanized infantry, self-propelled field artillery and air defense operation. As with other courses, the emphasis here is on small unit ground combat operations. This emphasis on small units allows the cadets an opportunity to practically apply military principles learned in the classroom during the plebe year.

By the end of the summer, the third class cadets are much more knowledgeable about the Army way. They have experienced some of the environments in which small Army units are placed, and they have experienced some of the challenges which face a junior officer and have developed their skills toward a future assignment in the Regular Army.

As the school year begins the sophomore cadets continue their military training in the classroom. The professional program for the third class cadet again consists of two required courses. First semester brings a course entitled Combined Arms Operations. Essentially a study of tactics, this course provides the cadet with a basic understanding of the employment of the company combined arms team. It

also prepares the cadets for either the Cadet Troop Leader Training Program or the Drill Cadet Program, which are part of the second class summer training efforts. This Combined Arms Operations course emphasizes the mission organization and capabilities of the elements of the combined arms team. These specific elements include combat, combat support and service support. Throughout the course, the role of the non-commissioned officer in army operations is a primary focus. Discussion of platoon leader duties in both field and garrison situations helps prepare the third class for summer training assignments with operational units of the Army.

The second military science course of the Third class year is Terrain Analysis. This course gives the cadet the opportunity to gain a basic knowledge of earth sciences. In addition, the course provides an introduction to map and aerial photo interpretation techniques. The focus of the class is to provide the basic knowledge necessary for cadets to prepare terrain analysis of actual (simulated) military operational sites. The cadets utilize maps and imagery interpretation techniques to study a diverse range of landscapes. By the end of the course each cadet participates in the preparation of a detailed area analysis of a selected location.

May brings the end to the second year at the Military Academy. Graduation week ceremonies include the promotion of the classes and our third class cadets become juniors—second class juniors at the Military Academy. The new second class gets a well-earned June vacation.

July comes swiftly and the new second class must report for the summer training program, which splits the class into groups for training assignments. Half the class will participate in Cadet Troop Leader Training. Selected cadets will join Regular Army units in Germany, Panama, Alaska, Hawaii, Korea and the United States for practical experience as junior officers. The other half of the class will participate in the Drill Cadet Program. These individuals will train the Army's new enlisted recruits at one of eight training centers in the United States.

'Bang! You're dead.' In the cadets' second summer, they're assigned one of two major training categories—Cadet Troop Leader Training (CTLT) or the Drill Cadet Program (DCP). After this 'Leader Training,' they report to special Army training centers like this cadet *(left)* in Airborne training at Fort Benning, Georgia. The device on the end of his rifle emits a light beam that tells both marksman and target when a 'hit' has been scored. Other Army training courses include helicopter assault training *(below)* at Fort Campbell, Kentucky.

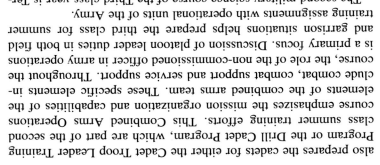

Second-summer cadets may be chosen for the Cadet Troop Leader Training (CTLT) program, to gain practical experience as junior officers in US Army units at locations around the globe, and may participate in such Regular Army training exercises as the 1985 Reforger (Return of Forces to Germany) war games *(above left and below right).* After their senior year, they become commissioned Army officers—eligible for Ranger training *(lower left),* and perhaps commanders of small units, including advance patrols such as the one shown *above.*

Following this leadership training, the class is reunited and will receive assignments to various military specialty training courses. Some cadets will receive flight training at Fort Rucker, Alabama. Others will travel to Panama for jungle training. Some will be sent to Alaska for northern warfare training, while others will participate in airborne and ranger training at Fort Benning, Georgia. A few will receive helicopter assault training at Fort Campbell, Kentucky. Finally, in one of the toughest courses of all, some will journey to Colorado for SERE school. SERE is an acronym for Survival, Evasion, Resistance and Escape.

No matter what the training ground, second class cadets generally agree that the experiences of their third summer at the Academy are among the most valuable. Certainly they are the most exciting of their military career to that point.

The school year brings yet another military science program. The third year military science course is entitled Army Systems Manage-

From the 'Corps of Invalids' of the Revolutionary War to Major Sylvanus Thayer's strengthening of morale through 'tightening up' discipline both on the parade field—which is proudly evidenced by this modern Brigade Staff unit, shown *above* at the graduation ceremonies—and in the minds of the officers-to-be, West Point's guardianship of tradition embraces old *(left)* and new.

ment and Public Speaking. Really a two-part course, the major focus is to describe a systems approach to organizations in general, and then apply this concept to the Army. All of the Army's functional subsystems are examined from a platoon leader level. These subsystems include such elements as personnel, training, supply and maintenance. Systems management techniques are also used to examine the Army's total structure and identify the criticality of the functional subsystems to the actual readiness of forces.

In this course cadets also receive instruction in the skills of public speaking. This section of the course emphasizes the importance of communication within an organization. Once the cadets have analyzed the Army through the eyes of a systems approach, they are better able to understand the need for clear communication skills. The public speaking instruction is reinforced by the use of films of famous speeches, and by classroom exercises. Then, by speaking to classmates in various forums, cadets are able to practice the speaking techniques they have learned.

The Senior year at the Academy is the best and worst—in that after three years of hard work the students are now first class cadets, yet the year until graduation seems almost as long as all three of the previous years combined. First class cadets effectively run the day-to-day program at the Academy; they form the student government; they instruct the new fourth class in the basic operation of the Academy; and they are almost through the four year program. The seniors are the leaders of the Corps of Cadets: they have significantly more privelege and latitude than do any of the more junior members of the Corps, yet they also have much greater responsibility.

Summer training is something of a repeat for the first class. These cadets find themselves back at Camp Buckner on the grounds of West Point, with the difference that, this time, it is they who are running things. The first class is responsible for much of the training of the third class cadets at the Camp Buckner summer program, and they are also on the 'good' side of Beast Barracks: the new group of plebes arriving in July are taught about the Academy and the ways of the Army by the first class.

In some ways a circle has formed. The first class teaches the lower class so that when they move up they too may pass on their knowledge. In a sense the first class summer is easy because they have been through it all before; but, in another sense, this last summer at the Academy is more demanding. A very keen sense of historical responsibility is born of the fact that now the first class must use their training and leadership skills to competently teach another class, and that class must go on to do the same for a future class, and so on.

With the start of the school year, the first class cadets are selected to fill leadership positions, ranging from that of Commander of the 4400 member corps to those of leaders of 44-member platoons, as well as various other staff positions which manage the activities of the Corps of Cadets. Again the new seniors are challenged to use their skills for planning, organizing and (most important) leading.

The Brigade color guard is shown *below* **during a parade drill on 'the Plain.' Yearly marching time has been cut 70 percent to give cadets more time for study and modern battle training.** *Right:* **These newly arrived students are being informed of their status as plebes—of which there are two kinds: 'beasts' who have not yet been recognized by an upperclassman, and 'human beings' who, after an upperclassman closely scrutinizes their obedience to upperclassmen and the Academy regimen in general, receive the recognition handshake.**

Left: Cadets await their diplomas in this graduation day photo. Throughout their West Point education, their every clothing choice has been dictated by a system of clothing-coded signal flags flying at various locations on campus. *Above and overleaf:* This is the famous 'hat throw,' which signifies these cadets' impending departure as graduates and their commissioning as Army second lieutenants— off with the old, on with the new. *Right:* Vice President George Bush is shown attending the West Point graduation ceremony.

The final military science course taken by the cadets is a most practical one. This is Army Service Orientation, which is intended to assist each cadet in making the transition from cadet at the Military Academy to second lieutenant in the Regular Army of the United States. This course includes a series of lectures, panel discussions and conferences designed to assist the cadet in selecting an appropriate branch of service within the Army. (To ensure that all branches receive an appropriate number of new officers from each graduating class, the Department of the Army establishes quotas governing the maximum and minimum number of cadets who may be commissioned in each branch.) This orientation training assists the cadets in requesting an initial assignment and provides information on such topics as personal finance, travel and personal affairs.

Completion of the course marks an end to a cadet's stay at the Military Academy. May brings graduation and commissioning. After four long years the cadet becomes an officer in the Army of the United States, leaving the Academy for a first duty station and the start of a career. Graduation also means having earned a bachelor of science degree: we will now look at what it takes to earn a degree at the United States Military Academy.

THE ACADEMIC LIFE OF A CADET

Cadets entering the United States Military Academy face a difficult challenge. Not only must they successfully complete the professional curriculum required for commissioning, but they must also undertake the courses leading to an accredited bachelor's degree.

The United States Military Academy education is based on a 'whole person' concept. Graduates of the Academy must be enlightened leaders with critical, resourceful creative minds. The Academy provides the broad college education demanded by the military profession, while at the same time maintaining an edge of academic specialization which is comparable to that of civilian universities in the United States.

Standard academic courses provide an essential core of general knowledge in the fields of arts and sciences. These general education courses are designed to provide each cadet with a critical, problem solving method. Advanced required courses provide educational depth, while electives allow the individual cadet to focus on specific areas of interest. This focus becomes the individual's major course of study if pursued to that end.

The classes themselves are in some ways unique to the Military Academy. To ensure the best opportunity to learn and develop, class size is limited to from 12 to 16 cadets. This assures the student's individual participation as well as sufficient instructorial attention to the student; indeed, the student to faculty ratio for core courses is 15 students for each faculty member.

To keep the students interested, they are grouped into classes by ability. In this way the faculty may concentrate on whatever a *group* needs rather than try to balance the needs of a wide range of student talents. This grouping, with periodic adjustment as needed, allows the instructor to speed or slow the pace of the course in accordance with the needs of the student group.

Small class size encourages cadets to participate in all of their classes and allows frequent critical evaluation. If a student does not completely understand the material presented during a particular lecture, the cadet may request tutoring (the Academy calls it additional instruction). Tutoring in any academic subject takes place on the same day that the cadet requests. There are no restrictions on this tutoring: a cadet may be at the 'top of the class' and still receive tutoring.

Now, before we look more deeply into the academic life of a West Point Cadet, we'll pause to consider some of the facilities which make up the learning environment. Only those schools with an excellent resource facility (aka 'library') can claim excellence in education. Cadets can rely on the Military Academy library for both

Left: **President Ronald Reagan is shown *here* in an award ceremony during West Point graduation day. Special award presentations are not likely to be included in the main graduation ceremony. *Above:* Cadets have access to more than 500,000 volumes at the Academy library, which is excellent and comprehensive in the science, mathematics and military subject areas, and is becoming increasingly strong in the liberal arts. The library also avails students of an extensive audio visual department, and plenty of assistance.**

academic research as well as for recreational reading, and while the library is a good liberal arts resource, it is most comprehensive in the areas of science, mathematics and military subjects. Users of the Academy library have access to more than one-half million volumes and approximately 2000 magazines and newspapers from all over the world. New plebes are given a detailed library orientation—intended to open the door to independent research—by the staff. The library staff is attuned to the needs of the cadets and are there to help the students use the various library catalogs and research tools effectively. The library also provides the cadets with an extensive audio

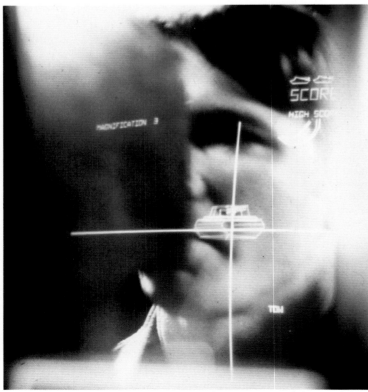

Above: **As well as having computer study equipment** *(left),* **the library contains an extensive art collection, including portraits (some of which are seen above these student's heads) of Jonathan Williams, the Academy's first Superintendent—by Thomas Sully; Thomas Jefferson, third president of the United States, who signed the Congressional bill on 16 March 1802 formally creating the Academy—by Thomas Sully; the famous portrait of George Washington by Gilbert Stuart; and other significant personages. Just south of the Plain, adjoining Bartlett Hall, the new Academy Library** *(right)* **was built in 1961-62 on the same site as the old (built in 1841) Library.**

video collection including almost 9000 records, television cassettes and tapes.

A second important Academy facility is the school's computer operation. The cadets all receive an introduction to computers in their first academic year. Following this course the students have access to an instructional computer system by way of more than 200 terminals located throughout the campus. In addition, the academy has large remote-terminal laboratories located in each academic building. These terminal laboratories provide the opportunity for instructors to conduct in-class 'hands-on' computer instruction. There are also nine remote-terminal laboratories located in the cadet barracks, thereby giving all cadets convenient access to the computers.

Beyond the large central computing facility, there are several main computers located within specific academic departments. Although these smaller computers are intended to support instructors and research efforts, the computers are available to the entire Corps of Cadets.

The Academy has extensive computer facilities comprised of more than 200 terminals distributed throughout the campus and terminal laboratories in each academic building. Having both 'hard data' *(above)* and imaging *(below)* capabilities, computers are increasing in importance as military and instructional aids. *Right:* Edwin E 'Buzz' Aldrin graduated from West Point in mechanical engineering; got a Doctor of Science degree in Astronautics from MIT; participated in the Gemini 12 solar eclipse photo mission of 11 November 1966; and was the Lunar Module pilot of the epochal Apollo 11 Moon landing on 20 July 1969. Graduate school is assigned duty for many West Point graduates. *Overleaf:* A cadet relaxes in his quarters with a friend from 'back home.'

The computer age is here and the Military Academy's focus will ensure that every cadet has ample opportunity to learn and work with computers. In fact, the Academy has purchased more than 100 personal computers in order to promote the use and understanding of computer systems. Current cadets who are interested have an excellent opportunity to use the computer for study, or even recreational, use. Future cadets will each receive a personal computer intended to aid them in their studies. These computers will be kept by the cadets after graduation and may be used throughout their military careers.

Junior and Senior cadets (that is those of the second and first class) have the opportunity to conduct academic research at the Academy's Science Research Laboratory. These research efforts are conducted in conjunction with specific academic departments, and range from work in the Social Sciences to Physics to engineering. The Science Research Laboratory gives Academy students the opportunity to significantly improve their knowledge of a given field of endeavor.

Considering the Academy's combination of library, computer facilities and research laboratory, the cadets of the United States Military Academy have every opportunity to achieve academic excellence.

The actual academic program at the Academy is interesting. The curriculum is basically split into two parts. The two parts are similar to programs at most American universities. The students take a prescribed set of courses commonly called the core program, which is divided equally between arts and sciences and is designed to provide the cadets with a solid general education. The core curriculum contains the following courses: two years of mathematics; computer science; one year of chemistry; one year of physics; electrical engineering; one year of mechanics; one year of civil, electrical, nuclear or general engineering (depending on track); literature; one

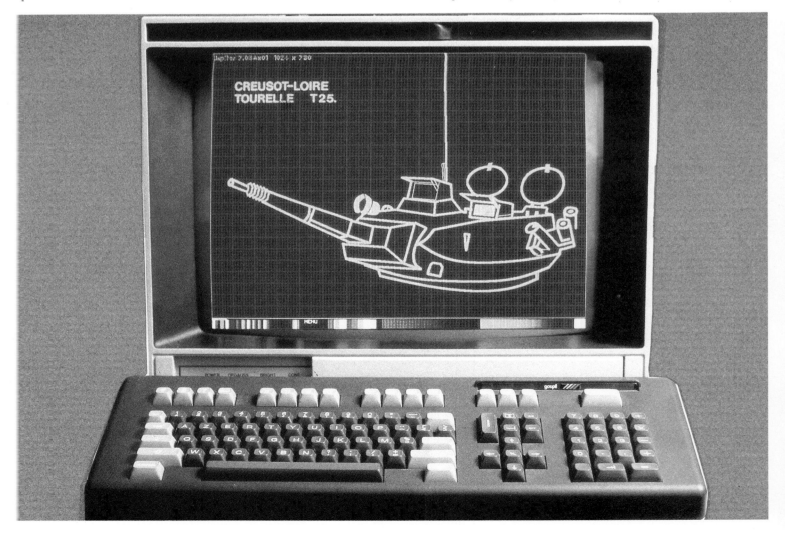

The statue of George Washington *(above)* on the Plain, near Thayer Road is a replica of the one in Union Square in New York City. Some say he is warning cadets away from the parade grounds. *Left:* Astronaut Michael Collins (West Point graduate and veteran of the Gemini 10 and Apollo 11 space missions) is shown aboard an Apollo 11 Moon mission training mockup. He is standing in the docking tunnel between the Command Module (which he piloted) and the Lunar Module.

year of English; two years of a foreign language; general psychology; one year of history; one year of law; one year of military history; a year and one-half of economics, political science and international relations. Overall, there are courses devoted to the social sciences and humanities; 15 courses devoted to mathematics, sciences and humanities; and 15 courses devoted to mathematics, sciences and engineering. The second part of the curriculum is essentially an elective sequence which fulfills either a cadet's interest area or meets the requirements for a degree with a specific major.

More than 90 percent of United States Military Academy graduates attend graduate school at some point in their career. The design of the core and electives program is set to prepare the cadets for further education.

Within the core and electives program, there is also what is known as the dual track program. The core curriculum consists of 32 courses which are considered essential to fulfilling the general knowledge requirement of each cadet. The core must also provide support for a cadet's choice of major. With this in mind, several core courses are offered in slightly different versions which relate to a program track. Essentially there are two tracks of study available. These are the mathematics-science-engineering track and the humanities-public affairs track. The selection of a track by a cadet is the starting point for the eventual selection of a major.

Between the two tracks there are almost 30 fields of study and 16 optional majors. Most cadets will choose a field of study in prepara-

Above: Teamwork is important in all aspects of Academy life. Chemistry labs and intricate equations are part of today's military officer training, as well-roundedness is essential to the leaders of an increasingly complex and sophisticated Army. The blackboard demonstration system *(right)* is an Academy tradition grounded in the belief that a problem is more accurately apprehended if presented in its totality. It is a legacy left to the Academy by Claude Crozet—appointed West Point Professor of Engineering on 6 June 1816.

tion for graduation. In effect, this choice means that a cadet will graduate with a professional military major with an academic specialization. Some cadets choose to have a specific major on their degree. These cadets must follow a prescribed series of classes which allows for a more in-depth study of a field. The program difference between a field of study and a major is relatively simple: each cadet has a total of 12 elective courses available for either field of study or major; should a cadet choose a field of study, then 10 electives must be devoted to that field. On the other hand, cadets who select a major must devote all 12 electives in pursuit of that field of interest.

In the mathematics-science-engineering track there are eight optional majors from which cadets may choose. These majors are chemistry, civil engineering, computer science, electrical engineering, engineering management, mathematical sciences and engineering physics. For those interested in a mathematics-science-engineering track but who would rather have a 'professional' major with a field of study, there are the following areas of interest in addition to those already noted: applied science and engineering; computer science; nuclear engineering; operations research and basic sciences. Students who are interested in mathematics, the physical sciences and the practical applications of these fascinating disciplines will likely find one of these fields both interesting and appealing.

For those not so inclined to have a focus in the sciences, the humanities and public affairs track may be where their interests are. There are eight optional majors in this track. These are behavioral sciences; economics; foreign languages; geography; history; literature; management; and political science. Professional majors may choose from the above or one of the following fields of study: American studies; foreign area studies; humanities; military history; military studies; modern history; national security; public affairs; and philosophy. The humanities and public affairs track is intended to prepare future Army officers to be leaders by developing their skills in communications, languages and critical thinking.

Grading is accomplished on an 'A through F' grade range. These letter grades are converted to a numerical system, ranging from 4.0 for an 'A' down to 0.0 for an 'F.' The grade point average is computed based on all final course work completed.

In order to graduate, each cadet must fulfill several requirements during their four years at the Academy. A cadet must complete a minimum of 44 courses—an equivalent of approximately 139 credit hours—with a minimum grade point average of 2.0, and all cadets must successfully complete all core curriculum courses. Third, each cadet must complete the requirements for a field of study or a major. This means that their field of study or 12 major courses must be completed within a chosen specialty. Fourth, each student must complete all segments of the military training program. Finally, all cadets are required to complete the physical education program.

A cadet who fails a course is reported to the Academic Board. Based upon a Board decision, he or she may expect some form of action because of the failing grade. The possible range of actions are three. First a cadet may be placed on a probationary status; this permits the cadet to continue with the regular academy program, subject to certain conditions which may include repeating the entire failed course. Second, a cadet may be required to attend an academic summer session. Third, the cadet could be dismissed from the Military Academy. (A cadet who is dismissed for academic deficiency in a single subject is entitled to a reexamination. Successful reexamination will result in the cadet's readmission to the academy.) A cadet may, in a rare occurrence, be required to repeat an entire academic year.

We noted earlier that approximately 90 percent of all military academy graduates go on to attend graduate schools.

Two of the graduate programs available to Military Academy graduates involve medical and legal training. Up to two percent of each graduating class of the Academy may attend medical school immediately following graduation. The exact number of graduates selected will vary depending upon the qualifications of the applicants as well as the needs of the Army, and the graduate must be accepted

Left: **Colonel David R Scott (Academy class of 1954) flew on the Gemini 8 and Apollo 9 space missions. Commander of the Apollo 15 Moon mission, Scott was the seventh man to take a lunar stroll *(above),* and one of the first to operate the Lunar Roving Vehicle (LRV)—which was a significant feature of the Apollo 15 mission, as the increased mobility afforded by the LRV significantly increases the lunar surface area which can be explored by astronauts. Scott went on to a distinguished career in NASA administration. *Below:* A group photo of the female cadets of the West Point class of 1980.**

Since West Point's beginnings as a military engineering school, the scope of education and the possibilities open to Academy graduates have greatly increased, yet many engineering courses remain crucial to the Army endeavor: both civil and tactical constructions are important military activity. Engineering education *(above and below)* at West Point has been honed to a high degree of excellence. 'A science in itself,' structural engineering is important to both tactical *(right)*, and peacetime operations.

into an accredited medical school. There are two fully-funded sources that produce doctors for the Army. The first is the Uniformed Services University of the Health Sciences, and the second is the United States Army Health Professions Scholarship Program.

Aspiring lawyers must complete at least two years of active duty to become eligible for law school. Under provisions of the Judge Advocate General Funded Legal Education Program, roughly 25 Army officers per year may attend law school. Selection for law school eligibility is competitive among all active duty officers who may choose to apply.

Besides the above, if an individual elects to stay in the military following his initial commitment, he is usually sent to graduate school as part of his normal duty rotation. Qualified graduates are usually selected for post-graduate work at civilian universities between their fourth and 10th years of active military service. These programs are fully funded, and beyond that, some Academy graduates earn scholarships based on their work at West Point. The various available scholarships include the Rhodes, Olmsted, National Science Foundation, Daedalian, and Marshall scholarships.

Since 1923, more than 60 graduates of the United States Military Academy have been awarded Rhodes Scholarships to attend Oxford. Only three other schools in this country have had more Rhodes scholars in that time period. Selection for such a prestigious award is

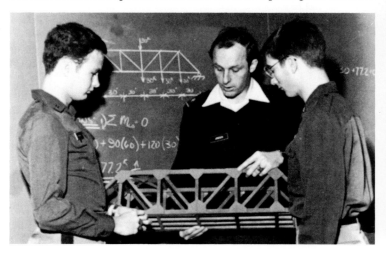

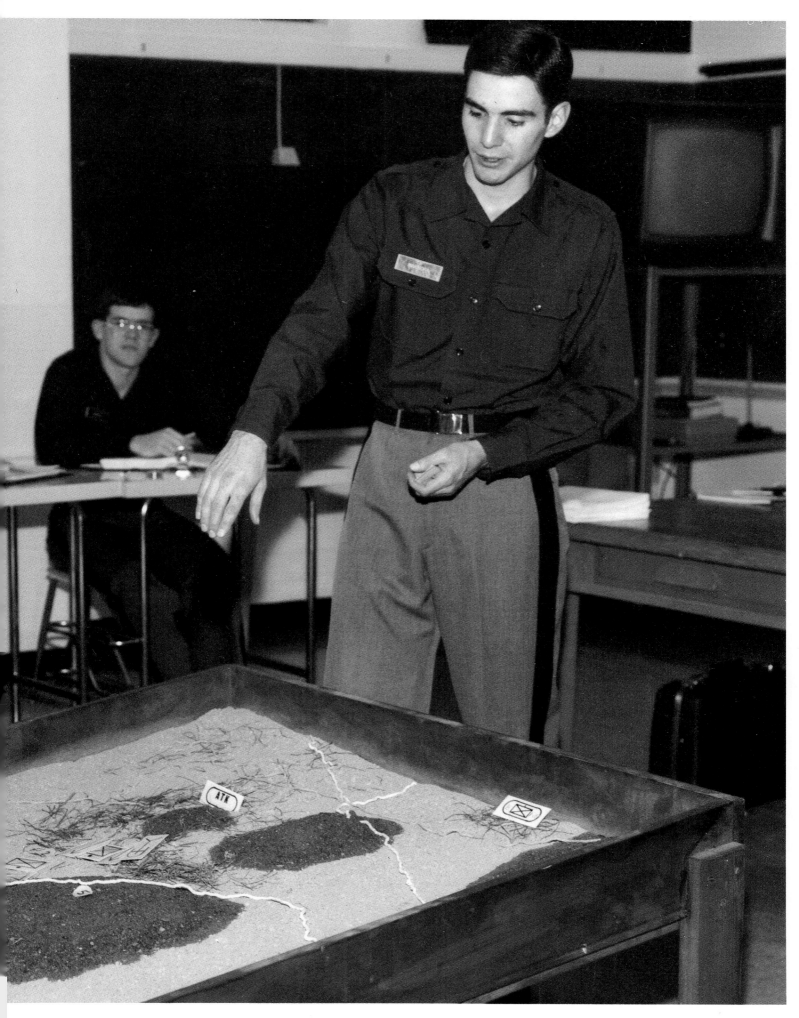

Engineering at the Academy covers a lot of ground. The Academy conducts a variety of courses in civil, electrical, general and nuclear engineering. Cadets in electrical engineering courses examine the electrical components of a jet engine *(above)*, and investigate the mysteries of circuitry *(below right)*. Academy computer systems are great problem solvers *(below left)* and terrific lecture hall aids *(above right)*—but some problems have 'a life of their own' *(below opposite)*. Overall, Academy course offerings encompass a wide range of liberal and applied arts subjects. Required courseloads are quite heavy, and added to the cadet's military courseloads, are tough enough to warrant sincere congratulations from fellow students upon graduation *(overleaf)*.

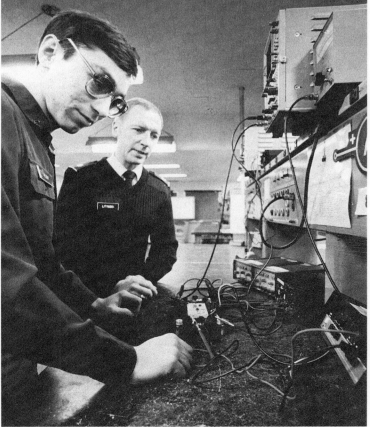

based upon criteria set down in Cecil Rhodes' will. The selection qualities are: intellectual excellence, strength of character, demonstrated leadership ability and athletic success. In his will, Rhodes expressed hope that scholars would 'esteem the performance of public duties as their highest aim.'

The Olmstead scholarship is awarded to Military Academy graduates to study for two years at a foreign university where a language other than English is spoken. The Olmstead Foundation considers junior officers for scholarships after they have served a minimum of three years of active duty. Scholastic ability, character and leadership while at the Military Academy are criteria for scholarship decisions.

Since 1961, 31 Military Academy cadets have been awarded National Science Foundation Graduate Fellowships. These fellowships are awarded annually and recipients are allowed to pursue graduate studies at the university of their choice.

The Hertz Foundation has awarded 23 fellowships to Military Academy graduates. These awards are intended for doctoral studies in the various disciplines of applied physical science. Candidates for the awards are qualified by academic performance, personal recommendations and interviews with Foundation board members.

There are four service academies in the United States (Army, Air Force, Navy and Coast Guard). The Daedalian Scholarships are of-

The core curriculem offers courses that are considered essential to graduation. Within that context, there are two tracks, both of which include core courses, yet offer emphases anticipatory to career choices. The two 'tracks' are: mathematics/ science/engineering, and humanities/public affairs. This engineering-track cadet *(above)* may be headed for a career as a communications officer, and perhaps as a mission specialist with NASA. *Right:* Computer imaging is very useful in engineering design applications.

fered to these four academies on an alternating basis. Every four years, the Order of Daedalians awards one scholarship to a graduate of the Military Academy. The scholarship provides a $2500 grant for advanced study in a field related to aerospace engineering.

The Marshall scholarship was established by the government of the United Kingdom. This scholarship is directed towards graduates of United States colleges and universities. Recipients of the awards receive two years of academic study leading to a British university degree. The Marshall scholarship selection committee looks for distinction of intellect and character in potential candidates. Undergraduate scholastic performance and other achievements are the evidence of these qualities.

Young people who enter the United States Military Academy can expect to complete a regular program of academic study and at the same time prepare for their future responsibilities as commissioned officers in the Regular Army of the United States. Yet, military and academic studies are only part of the program at the Academy: Each cadet must also have some sort of release from the pressure of study. Athletics and extracurricular activities are available to round out a cadet's program.

FREE TIME

The life of a cadet at the United States Military Academy is at least hectic. Although all cadet schedules are unique, we can at least profile a typical day. If the cadet is a plebe, the academic day begins with breakfast at 6:30 in the dining hall. This is a required activity for plebes and an optional event for all upperclass cadets. All cadets are required to be at the morning formation at 7:15. The day's first classes begin as early as 7:30 and run until noon. All cadets are expected at lunch formation at 12:20. Following lunch, classes start up again just after one o'clock and continue until 3:30. Dinner is served at 6:30 in the evening and evening study time is scheduled from 7:30 until 11:30, when taps sound. 'Lights out' is officially scheduled at taps, but cadets may choose to study as late as they wish.

The official day starts at about 6:30 and ends at about 11:30. With their day so completely scheduled, how or when do cadets have any time to do anything? The answer is that freetime is also a scheduled event. From 3:30 in the afternoon until the evening meal, cadets participate in athletics, extracurricular activities and (if necessary) additional instruction in subjects which they have lagged behind. The cadets learn quickly how to use their time well. Further, because the time pressure on the individual is extreme, the release from this pressure by way of athletics and extracurricular activities is welcomed.

The athletic program at the Military Academy is guided by the phrase 'every cadet an athlete, every athlete challenged.' Every cadet at the Academy must compete in intercollegiate, club or intramural sports. In addition, each cadet must participate in the school's basic physical education program. The faculty and alumni of the Academy have long felt that the value of an intense physical education program cannot be underestimated. Douglas MacArthur once remarked that 'The training in the athletic field, which produces in a superlative degree the attributes of fortitude, self control, resolution, courage, mental agility and, of course, physical development, is one completely fundamental to an efficient soldiery.'

The first level of activity which we will discuss is physical education as required for graduation. Sponsored by the Academy's Physical Education Department, the program has been designed around a three-part goal. First, the program is intended to develop useful habits of physical fitness which can then be applied by each cadet throughout his or her career. This orientation to fitness may also be used to train and instruct others in promoting a healthy style of living. Second, the Academy program is designed to develop endurance and strength to withstand the physical hardships expected of military life. Finally, the physical education program is designed to

Left: **If she looks a bit more reserved than most cheerleaders, perhaps it's because she's gunning for a generalship in the US Army. Cadets have a wide range of free-time activities to choose from, among which are sports, music, drama and attending the various performances given by other cadets engaged in these activities—such as the Army/Navy football game, an intense college football tradition of decades' standing. This lieutenant on leave *(above)* from active duty has decided to help his alma mater's cheerleading squad.**

develop the physical skills of the students while at the same time encouraging teamwork and competitive spirit. The training cadets receive helps them put the competition into perspective, and develops the confidence in them to attain goals both individually and through team work.

The Academy really doesn't need to do much to get cadets involved in the physical education program. The students who make it through the months of selection screening to attend the Military Academy are already a competitive group. The faculty at the Academy must channel that competitive energy into team building and

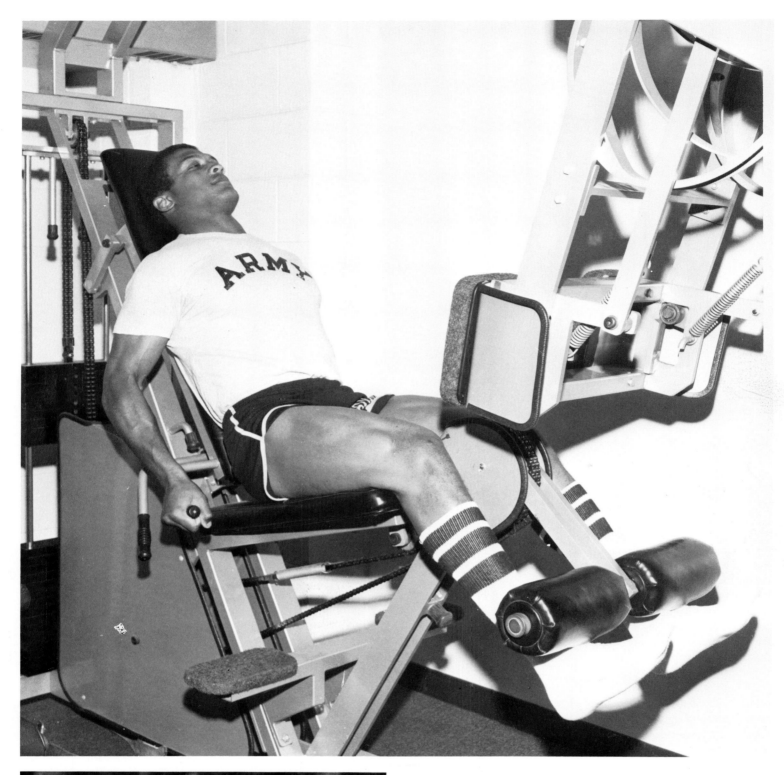

team work. Every aspect of life at the Military Academy is in place for a specific purpose and athletics is not an exception.

The Military Academy is, as we have seen, a very stressful place. In the physical education program, students can find a release from the day to day routine of the Academy and, at the same time, develop their skills in sports.

Women participate in the same physical fitness and physical education program as men. The physical education program begins during plebe summer and continues throughout the four year curriculum. Once involved, the cadets usually move right into intramural athletics. The intramural program begins at 3:40 every afternoon from Monday to Thursday. Normally each cadet competes in intramurals twice weekly. The Academy view of intramural sports is that they give every cadet a chance to build leadership, strength, coordination and endurance.

The Academy provides cadets with both staffing and equipment to guide their progress in physical culture. The cadets shown *above left and right* are developing strength and muscle tone in the Mitchie Stadium weight room. Academy intramural and varsity clubs participate in a variety of sports, including intercollegiate wrestling *(below, opposite)*. The Naval Academy mounts yearly assaults *(right)* against the Army football team, but their threat is small to the mighty Army black knight, atop his Army Mule *(overleaf)*.

The list of intramural sports is impressive and includes flickerball, full contact football, soccer, triathalon, track, basketball, boxing, handball, swimming, volleyball and more than a few others. For those interested in intercollegiate sports, teams from the Military Academy participate in quite a variety of sports. At the beginning of the school year there is football, of course, which generates the greatest amount of national recognition for the Academy—especially when the annual Army-Navy game is played.

Left: **The Commander-in-Chief's trophy, named in honor of the president of the United States, is awarded to the winner of the yearly round-robin football contest between the Military Academy and the Naval and Air Force Academies. The three sides of this trophy each bear the insignia and mascot of each of the academies, and is given to the overall winner until the next year's contests.** *Shown is the* **'Army side.'** *Above:* **Some of the Army team Heisman Trophy winners, and the dates on which they won the honor,** *left to right:* **Glenn Davis (1946), Felix Blanchard (1945) and Peter Dawkins (1958).** *Right:* **The West Point rugby squad counts bruises as badges of honor, the marks of many a 'hash.'** *Overleaf:* **Mitchie Stadium, the seat of West Point football glory.**

Army teams are fielded for many varsity sports, including basketball, baseball, track and field, swimming, soccer and lacrosse. In fact, the Military Academy sponsors about 30 varsity teams every year. The Academy athletic program of varsity level sports is financed by the Army Athletic Association, a non-profit organization composed of graduates and other Academy supporters.

For those not interested in varsity level sports, the Academy Club Sports program offers an opportunity to compete on an intercollegiate basis. Cadets who desire to compete have the opportunity to compete against other colleges, universities and clubs in more than 20 different sports. There are two levels of club sports: Athletic and Recreational. The difference between the two is simply the level of competitive and physical exertion.

On the Athletic Club Sports side we have bicycling, gymnastics, rugby, sailing, triathalon, volleyball and wrestling. The Recreational Clubs include bowling, karate, racquetball, riding and skeet shooting. In all of these club sports, the cadets are planners as well as participants. In this way the Academy continues to help the cadets develop their leadership skills.

Above: **Connie Kreski,** *Playboy* **magazine's Playmate of the Year, autographed photos for cadets in 1969.** *Below left:* **This huge historical mural in the cadet mess at Washington Hall depicts great military leaders ranging from Cyrus at Babylon in 538 BC to Joffre at the battle of the Marne in 1914 AD.** *Right:* **This Army 'black knight' dropped in on an Army football game via parachute.**

The Military Academy's athletic program is well supported by the school's various facilities. The gymnasium building contains five gyms, three swimming pools (one of which is olympic size) and a variety of other training rooms for squash, handball, weight training and contact sports. There is a football stadium, a hockey rink and a field house. Cadets also have use of baseball diamonds, a track, numerous other athletic fields, a ski slope, a golf course, tennis courts and some outdoor swimming pools.

As active as the cadets may be, many like the opportunity to do things in fields not related to sports. The Cadet Fine Arts Forum is the largest extracurricular group at the Military Academy. Cadets may pursue their interests in dance, theatre, photography, sculpture, painting, films and music through this activity. Others may wish to attend the several Military Academy Band concerts during the year, or get involved in cadet publications including their year book, *The Howitzer,* a magazine called *The Pointer* and a freshman handbook entitled *Bugle Notes.*

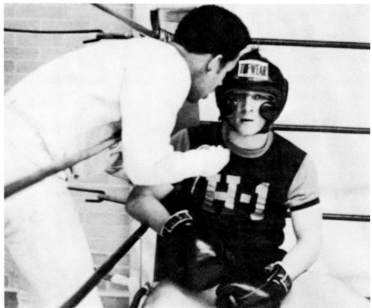

Things heat up during 'Navy Week,' when Navy needlers *(left)* visit West Point to harass and heckle in the week preceding the Army/Navy football game. Academy intramural activities—West Point's 'friendly rivalries'—range from squash to boxing *(above)*. Other cadet freetime activities include magazine production, dance, painting, films and *(below)* the Cadet Choir.

Other clubs at the Academy include such diverse interests as astronomy, engineering, electronics, geology and military affairs. Debating is a major interest for many cadets and more than six hundred participate in the Debate Council and Forum. There are Forum Councils in other areas such as the United Nations, domestic affairs, finance and the Student Conference on United States Affairs.

No matter how aggressive an individual may be, there are times when people need to reflect either singly or in groups. The Military Academy respects, and in fact encourages, cadet participation in religious organization. Services in the Protestant, Catholic and Jewish faiths are held each week in the Academy Chapel as well as in other prearranged locations on campus. A large group of cadets participate in teaching Sunday school and singing in the cadet choirs. Cadets

Left: Hearkening to another world—the Cadet Chapel's foundation was set level with the floodline of a glacier-era Hudson Valley flood; King Arthur's sword Excalibur hangs above its entrance; and carvings of the Quest for the Holy Grail extend around the clerestory. Some devotional services are performed with a Hudson River background *(right).* The MacArthur Monument *(above)* is located in front of Washington Hall—which also is the background in a December 1969 photo *(overleaf)* of cadet 'snowmanship,' perhaps part of the West Point emphasis on 'building the whole man?'

also serve as ushers and as members on Chapel boards to plan religious activities, as well as getting involved in religious retreats, Bible studies and prayer breakfasts if they choose. West Point religious activities provide a vital release for many cadets. The various chaplains on the staff are available to counsel (or just listen) if a cadet should need to talk.

Whatever a cadet's personal interests are, there is an opportunity to pursue them at the United States Military Academy, even though the Military Academy is a tough school, and students are challenged every step of the way—including just getting admitted to the program. Thus far we have examined several aspects of life at the Military Academy. We can now look to one last but all important question: How does one get into the Academy?

GETTING IN

One thing to say about the Military Academy is that the challenges which the students face are daunting. Indeed only a select few with outstanding ability and superior motivation even have a chance of making it through to graduation. For this reason, the admissions standards are quite high. At the Military Academy, scholastic ability, achievements in athletics and apparent leadership qualities are important factors for acceptance.

Academy standards are so difficult because cadets at the Military Academy are educated and groomed in the United States Army; and the expectations placed on those who graduate are very high.

Each year the Military Academy selects some 1300 cadets for the freshman class (which is also called the plebe or fourth class). Those admitted represent about 11 percent of all those who originally applied for admission. On the average, the Military Academy receives about 12,000 applications for admission. Of those, nearly 5400 are actually officially nominated to the Academy. Those nominated then must meet the actual entrance requirements for scholastic ability, medical qualification and physical ability. Usually only about half of those nominated make it through the admissions standards tests. And of the pool of 2400 applicants found to be fully qualified for admission, a little more than one-half will make it to the Academy.

The tough admission standard ensures that only the most qualified make it through, and of these the 'most qualified,' about 30 percent of each starting class will have left the Academy before completing the program. The admissions are tough for a purpose.

The competition for admission is keen, so it is never too soon to start preparing for the Military Academy: those interested in the Military Academy should consider their high school program carefully. The key to course work is that students should prepare for a difficult as well as demanding college program; students in high school should take college preparatory courses and strive to be in the top 20 percent of their class, as high school students who are below the top 40 percent will probably not qualify for the Academy. According to the Military Academy, about 83 percent of the students admitted for the class of 1988 (Academy freshmen in 1984) ranked in the top 20 percent of their high school classes.

The successful applicant's high school course work generally included the following: four years of high school mathematics including trigonometry (essential for the technical workload at the Academy); four years of English (future Army officers must be able to communicate both orally and in writing); two full years of a modern foreign language; and one year of high school chemistry and physics.

Everyone who is interested in the Military Academy should first

Left: **The average acceptee to the Academy has graduated in the top 20 percent of his high school class, has participated in one or more of his high school's extracurricular activities, and may have had some collegiate experience previous to attending the Academy. In addition to this, the students's eyesight must be superb—with some very slight exceptions—and must not have had corrective eye surgery.** *Above:* **The Soldier's Monument is near Mitchie Stadium, between Lusk Reservoir and Fort Putnam.**

consider whether they are qualified. Each candidate must be at least 17, but not yet 22 years old, by July 1 of the year of admittance. Each prospective cadet must be a United States citizen at the time of enrollment. There are exclusions to this requirement for foreign students who are nominated by agreement between the United States and another country. A third general consideration is that every prospective cadet must not be married or have a legal obligation to support a child or children.

Above: Cadet John Adams is shown in this 1968 photograph—167 years after his namesake, the second president of the United States warmly supported the creation of the Academy, but left the groundwork to Thomas Jefferson. *Right:* Flanked by a lieutenant major *(near)* and a full major, then-president of France Vincent Auriol is shown at West Point in 1951, taking in the Academy marching band *(right rear),* a special honor guard *(right),* the Central Cadet Barracks *(left)* and Bartlett Hall *(right). Overleaf:* On its hillside, the Cadet Chapel seems to rise above Washington Hall, despite the latter's huge 'wings.'

Everyone who is interested in the Military Academy will be asked to complete a precandidate questionnaire. The Academy would like to see these forms by the spring of the applicant's junior year of high school. This questionnaire is designed to be a first screening of applicants. The Military Academy will begin an applicant file, and prepare an initial evaluation of each potential candidate's background. This evaluation is shared with the future candidate. Once complete and reviewed, this file will be forwarded to the candidate's Congressional Representative and two State Senators for consideration. At this point a candidate's file will include the questionaire, the Academy evaluation, the results of a medical examination and any other information which has been forwarded by the applicant. All of this data will be of assistance to the Congressmen and Senators in appraising the applicant.

Each potential candidate for the Military Academy must take either the Scholastic Aptitude Test (the SAT) or the American College Testing Program (ACT) test. Although there is no rule on how soon a candidate may take one or both of these tests, they must be taken before February of the year of hoped-for admission to the Academy. There is such emphasis placed on these test scores that students interested in applying for admission are actually urged to take them in their junior year, as early testing helps the Academy and members of

Congress to make an unrushed decision on an applicant's candidacy. If a candidate takes these tests more than once, the scores from the tests taken after December of his or her junior year in high school are averaged by the Military Academy. This composite score is then used in evaluating an individual's scholastic abilities. For reference purposes, SAT scores of accepted applicants average about 1250 points while their ACT scores average about 55. In all, an applicant should show a good balance between language and mathematics scores.

Each applicant must be nominated by an official source. Nominations may come from ten official nominating sources. The first of these is Congress. United States Senators, Representatives, District of Columbia delegates to Congress and the Resident Commissioner

Above: **The visitor travelling 50 miles from New York City will likely be greeted by this south view of the Academy's massive educational facility and classroom center, Thayer Hall, which also houses the West Point Museum—crammed with military paraphernalia used by and against the US, including the first and second projectile loads fired in the epochal Civil War 'firing upon Fort Sumter.'** *Right:* **The Superintendent, chief executive of the Academy, shares these offices on the west side of the Plain with the Dean.**

of Puerto Rico may all nominate candidates to the Academy. There are some restrictions, however: each of these sources may only have five cadets attending the Academy at any one time, but each may make up to 10 nominations for a specific vacancy—in which case, a nominating official may sponsor an individual as the prime nominee and then nine alternates.

Not only the usual executive influence is exercised by US presidents, but each has 100 yearly personal appointments to make to West Point (as well as appointments to the US Air Force and US Naval Academies)—thus possibly determining the makeup of US military leadership for years to come. *Above:* Two turbulent US presidential decades are represented in one toast. *Left to right:* Richard Nixon, incumbent Ronald Reagan, Gerald Ford and Jimmy Carter. *Left:* The Cadet Chapel, just south of Fort Putnam, is seen *here* as viewed from the east. Academy graduate Sherwood Spring *(at right)* and Naval Academy graduate Bryan O'Connor were among the crew of the *Atlantis* (STS 61-B) Experimental Assembly of Structures in Extravehicular Activity (EASE) mission of 26 November 1985. *Overleaf:* The 'new' Cadet Chapel's construction was begun in 1906 by Superintendent Major Hugh Scott.

The President of the United States may make 100 nominations each year. However, these nominations must be children of career officers and enlisted personnel of the armed forces and the Coast Guard. 'Career' status for these nominations is defined as either continuous active duty for a period of at least eight years, or retirement from the military with pay.

The Vice President of the United States may sponsor five cadets attending the Military Academy at any one time. The candidates for this selection may come from anywhere within the United States.

Children of Medal of Honor Winners is a fourth category of official nominating sources. Unlike the three already discussed, there is no limit to the number of appointments in this particular category. Related to this is a nomination category for children of deceased or disabled veterans, and children of servicemen who are officially listed as either missing in action (MIA) or as prisoners of war (POW). A maximum of 65 appointments in this category may be at the Academy at any one time.

There are approved military preparatory schools throughout the country which may nominate individuals. Ten appointments are al-

Above: Lt General Henry H 'Hap' Arnold is shown *here* with Lee Gerlach of the Junior Air Reserve, an auxiliary of the Army Air Forces, in the early 1940s. Lt General Arnold went on to become the World War II commander of the Army Air Forces, and the only airman to attain a five-star rank. His years at the US Military Academy, however, were writ in mediocrity. Prankster and illicit fireworks engineer *par excellence,* he was in constant trouble. Upon entering the Regular Army, he became a follower of airpower visionary General Billy Mitchell and his native talent at last came to life. *Right:* The 'Long Gray Line.'

lowed each year and the nominations are made by the headmaster of each school.

The Governor of Puerto Rico; the Administrator of the Panama Canal Zone; and delegates to Congress from Guam, the Virgin Islands and American Samoa may each have nominees in attendance at the Academy. Guam and Puerto Rico are allowed one and American Samoa and the Canal Zone are each allowed two.

Two nominating categories are available for active duty Army personnel. The first is for regular enlisted personnel on at least one year of active duty. The second category is for the Army Reserve. Again, personnel must have compiled at least one year of service. For both of these categories there are 85 possible appointments, (170 in all) allowed each year.

The final nominating category is for the Army Reserve Officer Training Corps. In this category 10 appointments are allowed each year.

It was noted earlier that members of Congress may sponsor five cadets in attendance at the Military Academy at any one time. For each vacancy, the nominating source may select 10 candidates to fill the vacancy. Once this is done, the nominator may select a principal nomination with alternates, or all 10 may be forwarded to the Academy for ranking by the Admissions office. No matter how the congressional nominator opts to present nominations, the candidate on the list who is found to be best qualified for admission to the Academy will be appointed to fill the vacancy. The remaining nominees then become qualified alternates for admission. Each year the Academy selects several hundred alternates. This list of alternates is used

Above: The graduation day parade takes place on the Parade Grounds (aka 'the Plain'). *Below:* The happiness of graduation day precedes yet more hard work—either in direct military service, or in further educational career refinements, as dictated by each cadet's 'duty rotation,' ie how the Army can use them best. *Right:* The responsible future beckons with a sobering aspect.

to bring the size of an entering class up to planned levels (in other words, about 1300 individuals).

By the time a new class is selected, it has the following profile: Over 83 percent of the students ranked in the top 20 percent of their high school class. The class includes about 200 minority cadets.

Although long a 'male-only' school, since the Academy first went co-ed in 1976, women have done well. In meeting the need for women officers, the Military Academy admits about 160 women in each class. The competition is as keen for them as for men. More than 1800 women challenged for the 125 seats available in the class of 1988.

Nomination is only the first step on the way to gaining an appointment. Once a candidate has secured a nomination, it is time to take a very thorough medical examination. This complete physical is designed to ensure that, if admitted, each cadet will have the physical and mental strength needed to meet the demanding standards of the Military Academy program.

Although the criteria for this medical examination are exacting, most candidates who are in generally good health and who have normal vision can pass the physical requirements.

Left: **The Battle Monument was originally conceived as a monument to the officers and men of the Regular Army who fought in the Civil War. Its granite shaft is 46 feet long. The figure of 'Fame' atop the shaft and the memorial plaque and other bronze decorations were made from fifty bronze guns (captured from the Confederates) donated by Congress. The monument is set at Trophy Point, near the northern extreme of Thayer Road, overlooking the Hudson.** *Above:* **A cadet assists in Mitchie Stadium weight room training.**

The requirements for normal vision are strict. Corrected visual acuity of 20/20 is a basic requirement for admission. There are waivers, but some eye standards are not open for the possibility of waiver: candidates who have had vision corrective surgery techniques such as radial keratotomy will not be admitted to the Academy. All prospective United States Army Officers must have normal color vision: there are no waivers for applicants who are unable to distinguish vivid red and green.

Once a candidate has passed the medical examination, the focus shifts to physical ability: all candidates must pass a Physical Aptitude Examination. This test is designed to evaluate a candidate's physical strength, coordination and endurance. There are four parts to the test. First is an upper body strength test: men must perform pullups and women are required to do flexed arm hangs from a pull-up bar. The next test, a standing long jump, is really nothing more than jumping as far forward as possible from a standing start. The next test is a basketball throw from a kneeling position. The fourth test is a 300-yard shuttle run.

The Physical Aptitude Examination is not particularly difficult for most candidates. However, we must remember that this is only a qualifying examination. The real physical test of strength and endurance will come if a candidate is selected for admission. The plebe summer is itself very demanding from a physical standpoint. From the very first day of work, the new plebes are taxed. To adequately prepare, candidates should look beyond the Physical Aptitude Test and work on a total conditioning program. This includes running, strength exercises, swimming a minimum of 100 yards and performing many repetitions of pushups and pullups.

Individuals who successfully make it past the various hurdles are now placed in a pool of potential selectees. After months of preparation, it all comes down to awaiting acceptance or rejection. Offers of appointment to the Military Academy begin about mid-October, fully seven months prior to plebe summer. The offers continue through June. Those making the grade can look forward to July and the famous plebe summer.

By the time the class is filled, only about 10 percent of the original applicants have made the grade. Over 100 of those freshmen have had at least one semester of college work. Fifty are children of Academy alumni. Most have achieved some sort of high school honors; 30 percent have been class or student body officers. More than half have been elected to the National Honor Society. Almost 90 percent have received varsity letters and one-half of them have been

Below: **An honor guard on graduation day. Long past its use in regular warfare, the saber is still the symbol of military command.** *Right:* **Cadets make the transition to officers in the Regular Army in this swearing-in ceremony. Their relatives watch proudly as these young men agree to shoulder the heavy responsibility of leadership in the armed forces. They, in turn, may some day sit watching as their own children enact the same ritual.**

team captains. And more than 20 percent were involved in high school public speaking and debating societies.

Once accepted to the Academy, each individual must sign an agreement by which they basically promise to fulfill five conditions. Each appointee must state his intention to complete the course of instruction at the Academy; upon completion each will accept an appointment and serve active duty as a commissioned officer in the Regular Army for a minimum of five years beginning immediately after graduation; each individual will accept a commission in the Reserve components of the Army if a regular commission is not offered; if any of the three points already covered are not fulfilled then the individual will serve in an enlisted capacity for not more than four years; and each appointee must agree to reimburse the United States for the cost of education received at the Military Academy if they fail to complete the period of active duty outlined in the contract.

The United States Military Academy represents a commitment to four full years of challenge and discipline. The mission of the Academy is 'to educate, train and inspire young Americans to become professional officers in the Regular Army.' The program is tough and the strain on individuals is heavy, but the men and women who make it through are some of the best that this nation's youth has to offer. The Regular Army officers who have graduated from the Military Academy are leaders of one of the world's most sophisticated armed forces.

Left: **The Cadet Color Guard marches on the Parade Ground, under the benedictory air of the Washington Monument, seen** *here* **against the expanse of Washington Hall.** *Above:* **Cadet camaraderie is likely to outlast graduation, as friends in different service areas 'keep in touch.'** *Below:* **Captain Conovan elucidates a problem for Cadet Palmer.** *Overleaf:* **With a poetic sweep of the arm, an upperclassman waxes discursive with a fellow, extolling this view of West Point's North Dock Cove.**

MACARTHUR'S VIEW

Douglas MacArthur was, as we noted earlier, once a Superintendent of the Military Academy. Many years later as he was leaving the Army, MacArthur presented one of the most inspirational speeches ever given at the Academy, on the occasion of his being given the Sylvanus Thayer Award:

'No human being could fail to be deeply moved by such a tribute as this. Coming from a profession I have served so long, and a people I have loved so well, it fills me with an emotion I cannot express. But this award is not intended primarily to honor a personality, but to symbolize a great moral code — the code of conduct and chivalry of those who guard this beloved land of culture and ancient descent. That is the meaning of this medallion. For all eyes and for all time, it is an expression of the ethics of the American soldier. That I should be integrated in this way with so noble an ideal arouses a sense of pride and yet of humility which will be with me always.

"Duty—Honor—Country." Those three hallowed words reverently dictate what you ought to be, what you can be, what you will be. They are your rallying points: to build courage when courage seems to fail; to regain faith when there seems to be little cause for faith; to create hope when hope becomes forlorn. Unhappily, I possess neither the eloquence of diction, that poetry of imagination, nor that brilliance of metaphor to tell you all that they mean. The unbelievers will say they are but words, but a slogan, but a flamboyant phrase. Every pedant, every demagogue, every cynic, every hypocrite, every troublemaker, and, I am sorry to say, some others of an entirely different character, will try to downgrade them even to the extent of mockery and ridicule. But these are some of the things they do. They build your basic character, they mold you for your future roles as the custodians of the nation's defense, they make you strong enough to know when you are weak, and brave enough to face yourself when you are afraid. They teach you to be proud and unbending in honest failure, but humble and gentle in success; not to substitute words for actions, nor to seek the path of comfort, but to face the stress and spur of difficulty and challenge; to learn to stand up in the storm but to have compassion on those who fall; to master yourself before you seek to master others; to have a heart that is clean, a goal that is high; to learn to laugh yet never forget how to weep; to reach into the future yet never neglect the past; to be serious yet never to take yourself too seriously; to be modest so that you will remember the simplicity of true greatness, the open mind of true wisdom, the meekness of true strength. They give you a temper of the will, a quality of the imagination, a vigor of the emotions, a freshness of the deep springs of life, a temperamental predominance of courage over timidity, an appetite for adventure over love of ease. They create in

Opposite: Douglas MacArthur graduated from West Point in 1903, made Brigadier General during World War I and was the Academy's Superintendent from 1912-22. The son of Civil War hero Arthur MacArthur, General Douglas MacArthur had what might be described as a military soul. He esteemed the character and value of the Army's regular troops whose monument is *above).*

your heart the sense of wonder, the unfailing hope of what next, and the joy and inspiration of life. They teach you in this way to be an officer and a gentlemen.

And what sort of soldiers are those you are to lead? Are they reliable, are they brave, are they capable of victory? Their story is known to all of you; it is the story of the American man-at-arms. My estimate of him was formed on the battlefield many, many years ago, and has never changed. I regarded him then as I regard him now—as one of the world's noblest figures, not only as one of the finest military characters but also as one of the most stainless. His name and fame are the birthright of every American citizen. In his youth and strength, his love and loyalty he gave . . . all that mortality can give. He needs no eulogy from me or from any other man. He has written his own history and written it in red on his enemy's breast. But when I think of his patience under adversity, of his courage under fire, and of his modesty in victory, I am filled with an emotion of admiration I cannot put into words. He belongs to history as furnishing one of the greatest examples of successful patriotism, he belongs to posterity as the instructor of future generations in the principles of liberty and freedom; he belongs to the present, to us, by his virtues and by his achievements. In 20 campaigns, on 100 battlefields, around 1000 campfires, I have witnessed that enduring fortitude, that patriotic self-abnegation and that invincible determination which have carved his statue in the hearts of his people. From one end of the world to the other he has drained deep the chalice of courage.

As I listened to those songs of the glee club, in memory's eye I

Above: **The MacArthur Monument, dedicated in 1969, presents him in a typically commanding yet meditative pose—surveying the situation, and about to issue a comment or command. His words uttered upon receiving the Academy's Sylvanus Thayer Award for excellence are etched in the granite surrounding him.** *Right:* **Bright young people of all sorts enter the Academy, but the ones who stay are those who respond enthusiastically to challenge.**

could see those staggering columns of the First World War, bending under soggy packs, on many a weary march from dripping dusk to drizzling dawn, slogging ankle-deep through the mire of shell-shocked roads, to form grimly for the attack, blue-lipped, covered with sludge and mud, chilled by the wind and rain; driving home to their objective and, for many, to the judgement seat of God. I do not know the dignity of their birth but I do know the glory of their death. They died unquestioning, uncomplaining, with faith in their hearts and on their lips the hope that we would go on to victory. Always for them, "Duty—Honor—Country"; always their blood, sweat and tears as we sought the way and the light and the truth.

And 20 years after, on the other side of the globe, again the filth of murky foxholes, the stench of ghostly trenches, the slime of dripping dugouts, those boiling suns of relentless heat, those torrential rains of devastating storms; the loneliness and utter desolation of jungle trails, the bitterness of long separation from those they loved and cherished, the deadly pestilence of tropical disease,

the horror of stricken areas of war; their resolute and determined defense, their swift and sure attack, their indomitable purpose, their complete and decisive victory—always victory. Always through the bloody haze of their last reverberating shot, the vision of gaunt, ghastly men reverently following your password of "Duty—Honor—Country."

The code which those words perpetuate embraces the highest moral laws and will stand the test of any ethics or philosophies ever promulgated for the uplift of mankind. Its requirements are for the things that are right, and its restraints are from the things that are wrong. The soldier, above all other men, is required to practice the greatest act of religious training—sacrifice. In battle and in the face of danger and death, he discloses those divine attributes which his Maker gave when he created man in his own image. No physical courage and no brute instinct can take the place of the Divine help which alone can sustain him. However horrible the incidents of war may be, the soldier who is called upon to offer and to give his life for his country is the noblest development of mankind.

You now face a new world—a world of change. The thrust into outer space of the satellite, spheres and missiles marked the beginning of another epoch in the long story of making—the chapter of the space age. In the five or more billions of years the scientists tell us it has taken to form the earth, in the three or more billion years of development of the human race, there has never been a greater, a more abrupt or staggering evolution. We deal now not with things of this world alone, but with the illimitable distances and as yet unfathomed mysteries of the universe. We are reaching out for a new and boundless frontier. We speak in strange terms: of harnessing the cosmic energy; of making winds and tides work for us; of creating unheard synthetic materials to supplement or even replace our old standard basics; of purifying sea water for our drink; of mining ocean floors for new fields of wealth and food; of disease preventatives to expand life into the hundreds of years; of controlling the weather for a more

'We deal not with things of this world alone, but with the illimitable distances and as yet unfathomed mysteries of the universe.' General Douglas MacArthur's words reveal wisdom that challenges the young of any age. Resolution and faith that something well may come of one's seemingly small efforts is the impetus to meet the challenge of the unknown—as the future of these West Point graduates *(left and below)* becomes manifestly that 'new world' of 'strange terms' of which MacArthur spoke so eloquently.

Above right: **West Point Academic Dean, Brigadier General Frederick A Smith Jr** *(with black tie)* **and West Point Superintendent, Lieutenant General Willard W Scott Jr** *(far right)* **present cadets with their commissions and degrees—and congratulations in this graduation ceremony photo.** *Left:* **A similar ceremony, with Dean Smith** *at center* **and Superintendent Willard** *at right.* **Various dignitaries sit under the canopy** *at rear* **and the Corps of Cadets is in the** *foreground. Above:* **Graduates are shown** *here* **being sworn in as US Army second lieutenants.**

equitable distribution of heat and cold, of rain and shine; of space ships to the moon; of the primary target in war, no longer limited to the armed forces of an enemy, but instead to include his civil populations; of ultimate conflict between a united human race and the sinister forces of some other planetary galaxy; of such dreams and fantasies as to make life the most exciting of all time.

And through all this welter of change and development, your mission remains fixed, determined, inviolable—it is to win our wars.

Everything else in your professional career is but corollary to this vital dedication. All other public purposes, all other public projects, all other public needs, great or small, will find others for their accomplishment; but you are the ones who are trained to fight: yours is the profession of arms—the will to win, the sure knowledge that in war there is no substitute for victory; that if you lose, the nation will be destroyed; that the very obsession of your public service must be "Duty—Honor—Country." Others will debate the controversial issues, national and international, which divide men's minds; but serene, calm, aloof, you stand as the nation's war-guardian, as its lifeguard from the raging tides of international conflict, as its gladiator in the arena of battle. For a century and a half you have defended, guarded, and protected its hallowed traditions of liberty and freedom, of right and justice. Let civilian voices argue the merits or demerits of our processes of government; whether our strength is being sapped by deficit financing, indulged in too long by federal paternalism grown too mighty, by power groups grown too arrogant, by politics grown too corrupt, by crime grown too rampant, by morals grown too low, by taxes grown too high, by extremists grown too violent; whether our personal liberties are as thorough and complete as they should be. These great national problems are not for your professional participation or military solution. Your guidepost stands out like a ten-fold beacon in the night— "Duty—Honor—Country."

You are the leaven which binds together the entire fabric of our national system of defense. From your ranks come the great captains who hold the nation's destiny in their hands the moment the war tocsin sounds. The Long Gray Line has never failed us. Were you to do so, a million ghosts in olive drab, in brown khaki, in blue and gray, would rise from their white crosses thundering those magic words "Duty—Honor—Country."

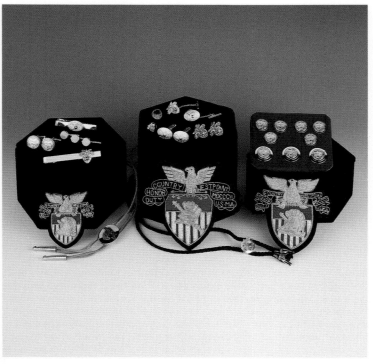

Below: **Chevrons and class ring. Class ranking (standing) has direct bearing upon promotion in the Regular Army. The number one cadet will get first promotional consideration among his 'generation' of Army second lieutenants; the second, second; down to the class 'goat,' who may be grey before he's promoted. Junior officers in the Regular Army are promoted by seniority until they attain general officership—and promotion by merit.** *Above:* **Alumni memorabilia are available from the Association of graduates.** *Left:* **More than memories are generated in the heartfelt bond of classmates on graduation day.**

This does not mean that you are warmongers. On the contrary, the soldier, above all other people, prays for peace, for he must suffer and bear the deepest wounds and scars of war. But always in our ears ring the ominous words of Plato, that wisest of all philosophers: "Only the dead have seen the end of war."

The shadows are lengthening for me. The twilight is here. My days of old have vanished tone and tint; they have gone glimmering through the dreams of things that were. Their memory is one of wondrous beauty, watered by tears, and coaxed and caressed by the smiles of yesterday. I listen vainly for the witching melody of faint

Above: Trophy Point in 1889, showing the confiscated Confederate cannon given the Academy by Congress to be melted down for the Battle Monument honoring the Union Civil War dead. *Below:* This is the view up the Hudson from Trophy Point to Bannerman's Island. *Right:* The Thayer Monument is shown in this 1920 photo as standing in front of the old Academy gymnasium, which was demolished for the construction of Washington Hall in 1929. 'The Father of the Military Academy,' Sylvanus Thayer graduated from West Point in 1808, fought in the War of 1812 and was an official observer of European military techniques and education until 1816. As a Brevet Major, he was appointed Superintendent of West Point by President James Monroe on 28 July 1817. He completely reorganized the sloppily-run, often nepotistically-governed officer's school into a model military educational institution. He instituted the educational, disciplinary and Honors systems used by the modern Academy; as well as creating several important administrative and academic posts; and last but not least, organized the Academy Band. He left the Academy in 1833, going on to do fortification work along the New England Coast. He died in 1872, and is buried in the West Point cemetary.

bugles blowing reveille, of far drums beating the long roll. In my dreams I hear again the crash of guns, the rattle of musketry, the strange, mournful mutter of the battlefield.

But in the evening of my memory, always I come back to West Point. Always there echoes and re-echoes "Duty—Honor—Country."

Today marks my final roll call with you, but I want you to know that when I cross the river my last conscious thoughts will be of The Corps, and The Corps, and The Corps.

I bid you farewell.'

MacArthur's speech describes what being a cadet at the Military Academy is all about. Those who make it through graduation will become the leaders of the Regular Army of tomorrow; the upholders and defenders of 'Duty—Honor—Country.'

Above and right: Silver and pewter ware bearing the Academy crest is available through the West Point Association of Graduates. As with many colleges and universities, there is an abundance of activities for alumni, including commemorative ceremonies every June at the Academy. The unique viewpoint inculcated into cadets stays with them lifelong, however, and these mementos are emblematic of an entire philosophy. The belief in 'Duty—Honor—Country' remains living even in the most hardened hearts, always waiting to spring forth anew.

INDEX

Below: 'And what sort of soldiers are these you are to lead?. . . the American man-at-arms. . . he gave all that mortality can give. . . His name and fame are the birthright of every American citizen. . .' *Overleaf:* '. . .This does not mean that you are war mongers. The soldier, above all other people, prays for peace, for he must suffer and bear the deepest wounds and scars of war.' One can almost hear the Cadet Chapel chimes further echoing General MacArthur's words: 'Duty— Honor—Country.'